Reading *Kingdom Come* is an invigorating reminder that the Bride of Christ has plenty to do to get ready for the wedding! And plenty to think about too. This book is an all-too-rare place where ministry and scholarship serve each other not only well, but with joy!"

ROBBIE F. CASTLEMAN, Assistant Professor of Biblical Studies and Theology, John Brown University

"Confronting the pervasive individualism of our culture, Allen Wakabayashi calls us to work out the implications of God's kingdom for our lives, communities and mission into the world. His commitment to see God change the world, and especially the university world, is contagious."

RICK RICHARDSON, author of *Evangelism Outside the Box*

"Unsatisfied with pie-in-the-sky escapism, Wakabayashi calls the evangelical community to fulfill its role as salt and light, pursuing justice, righteousness— even the glory of God—in all aspects of life in a fallen world."

RICHARD M. WEBER, Assistant Professor of Theology, Moody Bible Institute

"Allen Wakabayashi makes the case that God's Kingdom has come and signs of it are everywhere. We often miss it, though, because it is too radical, full of sacrifice and delight. Allen wants you to see the signs, take up your cross and join the parade."

ALEC HILL, president, InterVarsity Christian Fellowship/USA

"Allen Wakabayashi, himself well-apprised of the scholarly discussion, has performed a tremendous service by exploring the revolutionary implications of the crucial theme of the kingdom of God for the way we carry on our lives and our mission as followers of Jesus. This is an engaging, hopeful and refreshingly honest guide to life in the already-and-not-yet reign of God.

GARWOOD P. ANDERSON, Assistant Professor of Biblical Studies, Asbury Theological Seminary, Orlando

KINGDOM
COME

HOW JESUS WANTS TO

CHANGE THE WORLD

ALLEN M. WAKABAYASHI

IVP Books

An imprint of InterVarsity Press
Downers Grove, Illinois

InterVarsity Press
P.O. Box 1400, Downers Grove, IL 60515-1426
World Wide Web: www.ivpress.com
E-mail: email@ivpress.com

InterVarsity Press® is the book-publishing division of InterVarsity Christian Fellowship/USA®, a student movement active on campus at hundreds of universities, colleges and schools of nursing in the United States of America, and a member movement of the International Fellowship of Evangelical Students. For information about local and regional activities, write Public Relations Dept., InterVarsity Christian Fellowship/USA, 6400 Schroeder Rd., P.O. Box 7895, Madison, WI 53707-7895, or visit the IVCF website at <www.intervarsity.org>.

Scripture quotations, unless otherwise noted, are from the New Revised Standard Version of the Bible, copyright 1989 by the Division of Christian Education of the National Council of the Churches of Christ in the USA. Used by permission. All rights reserved.

Cover design: Rick Franklin

Cover image: Digital Vision

ISBN-10: 0-8308-2363-8
ISBN-13: 978-0-8308-2363-5

Printed in the United States of America ∞

Library of Congress Cataloging-in-Publication Data

Wakabayashi, Allen Mitsuo.
  Kingdom come: how Jesus wants to change the world / Allen Mitsuo
Wakabayashi.
    p. cm.
Includes bibliographical references.
  ISBN 0-8308-2363-8 (pbk.: alk. paper)
  1. Evangelistic work. 2. Kingdom of God. I. Title.
  BV3790.W313 2003
  231.7'2—dc22

                                                                                    2003016922

| P | 21 | 20 | 19 | 18 | 17 | 16 | 15 | 14 | 13 | 12 | 11 | 10 | 9 | 8 | 7 | 6 |
| Y | 21 | 20 | 19 | 18 | 17 | 16 | 15 | 14 | 13 | 12 | 11 | 10 | 09 | 08 | | | |

CONTENTS

PREFACE

"I think you need to write a book about the kingdom of God, Allen." My supervisor and friend, Greg Jao, was talking with me about our campus ministry at Northwestern University. Knowing that I had sought to build the ministry around my understanding of the kingdom of God, Greg thought I should try sharing what I've learned with a wider audience. Before too long, calls had been made to Andy Le Peau at InterVarsity Press, and now here I am, adding final touches to the book.

I first learned the biblical message of the kingdom of God back in the late 1980s, in a New Testament theology class with Dr. Julius Scott at Wheaton College Graduate School. He had us read George Eldon Ladd's *A Theology of the New Testament,* which taught me that the kingdom and its eschatology serve as a connective thread throughout the New Testament. Years later, in the context of ministry, William Abraham's *The Logic of Evangelism* transformed my paradigm of ministry and evangelism. Since then, the kingdom of God has become the foundation for my whole philosophy of ministry and understanding of the Christian life.

As I continued to read scholarly works in New Testament studies, I found a wealth of material that either dealt with Jesus' teaching on the kingdom or assumed a basic understanding of that message and its eschatology. Yet as I listened to people around me or read popular Christian books, I found an understanding of the kingdom to be sorely lacking. Jesus told us to seek first the kingdom of God (see Matthew 6:33). But how are we to seek it when we don't really understand what it is about?

I do not claim to know all that the kingdom of God is about, but I do feel that what God has taught me about the kingdom has transformed my whole outlook on and approach to life and service. So much scholarly literature on the subject of the kingdom exists, and many others understand the biblical message better than I do. Yet I hope that this book might serve to bridge the gap from the scholarly literature about the kingdom to the normal Christian who is not familiar with the academic material.

Furthermore, it is my hope that this book inspires readers to do further study on the kingdom. There is so much more about the kingdom than I can cover here; as I wrote the book there were many times I wanted to add chapters or go in new directions. And there were other times where I realized that I needed to do my own study to better understand certain concepts. Yet I knew that I needed to finish and keep the book to a reasonable size. I encourage you to continue your study of the kingdom of God by analyzing the parables, rereading the Synoptic Gospels and reading some of the resources listed in the bibliography.

I want to thank Greg Jao for initiating this writing project. Without his encouragement, this book would not have been written. Thanks also to Andy Le Peau at InterVarsity Press for all of his encouraging and constructive help for me, a first-time writer. Thanks to Dave Suryk, whose early conversations with me taught me a lot about the kingdom and encouraged me to keep going in my personal study. Also, many thanks to the staff and students of InterVarsity Christian Fellowship at Millikin University, Bradley University and Northwestern University, who have patiently endured my ramblings about the kingdom and helped me learn how to communicate what was going on inside my head and heart. In particular, thanks to my staff at Northwestern University: Sandra Van Opstal, Emery Silva and Kathy Khang.

Much love and many thanks to my wife, Diane, who has walked this journey with me and helped me understand what life in the kingdom is all about. Finally, I want to thank my parents, Gene and Kazue Wakabayashi. They named me Mitsuo, which in Japanese means "man of light." It expressed my mother's dream that I would grow up to be a man who stood for the light of Jesus. Together they raised me with that hope in mind. They raised me up to live for Jesus, they modeled what living for Jesus meant, and even today they continue to model for me what kingdom living is about. Humanly speaking, I believe that, more than anyone else, my parents are responsible for my continued faith in Jesus. I dedicate this book to them.

1

IS GOD REALLY OUT TO
CHANGE THE WORLD?

Is God out to change the world? Do you really believe that? Sometimes I wonder. How much do Christians believe that God is out to change the world? There are so many churches, so many Christians—reportedly two billion of us in the world. Yet the impact of the church on the world seems so small. Although many good things marked the turning of the millennium, the reality is that our world is full of incredible hardship, evil and pain. And the church of Jesus Christ, the community of people who know the hope of the world, often seems silent.

Sure, some people are doing wonderful things and some churches are engaging in radical ministry. Missionaries go to Siberia to preach the gospel, and Mother Teresa types are out there feeding the poor. But that's the problem, isn't it? It's only the radicals who are out there doing things that help to change the world.

For the most part, the rest of us maintain a quiet existence that fits easily into the mainstream. We don't rock the boat much as we flow downstream with the rest of society. We tell ourselves that we *are* being different. After all, we are active in our churches, we give money to missions causes, and we actively pray and read our Bibles.

I work on a college campus, and to a certain degree Christians there

do look different. They are *busy*. They are doing lots of Christian activities—Bible study groups, evangelistic outreaches, missions trips and so
forth. Yet the university around them goes on as usual, relatively unaf-
fected by their presence. I sometimes find it difficult not to grow dis-
heartened, because many Christians I see look just like everyone else,
and the world just goes on its destructive way.

I don't mean to be judgmental; I wonder these same things about myself. Do I look any different from my neighbors? I live a pretty comfortable, middle-class existence in Chicago. I drive a Honda Accord. If
people were to ask my neighbors about me, they'd probably say I was a
nice guy. I pick up after my dog, I say hi to the neighbors, and I don't
come home drunk on the weekends. So yeah, I'm a nice guy. But it's not
as if I am out in Calcutta feeding the poor or planting churches among
some unreached people group.

But isn't God out to change the world? The early church started off as
a little sect of Judaism made up of a ragtag bunch of nobodies preaching
about a crucified Messiah. Yet within a few generations, they changed
the face of the world as they went out preaching and living the gospel.
The entire Roman Empire was turned upside down. And ever since then,
there have been moments in history when Christians rose up and caused
society to take notice, and they changed the world—or, more accurately,
God changed the world through them. It was as if God had lit a match
in the church, and that was followed by an explosion of gospel activity
that permanently transformed society. People were converting left and
right, and as converts began walking in Jesus' ways the culture was dramatically altered to reflect the love and truth of the gospel.

Yet today the church seems so quiet. Shouldn't it be rocking the
world? In our part of the world, Christianity is not outlawed. We are free
to gather for worship and share our faith without fear of imprisonment.
And we are the heirs of a church that has contributed to the abolishment
of slavery, the pioneering of medicine and the growth of education. Yet
today the church does not seem to be turning our world upside down

with the gospel. Do we not believe that God is out to change the world?

I do not claim to have all the answers, but I do have a strong conviction that the church has lost its gospel moorings. We've lost the ability to *see* and *understand* the gospel in all of its depth and world-changing glory. It's as if our eyesight has slowly grown dim without our realizing it. As God points us to what he has done in Jesus Christ and calls us to live it out, we see only fuzzy pictures. Meanwhile, we believe that we've got it all figured out. We don't realize that we have severe myopia and desperately need some glasses. We need a vision adjustment.

It's not enough just to see and understand the gospel correctly; we must *live* the gospel correctly. However, our conceptual framework is the starting point. If we cannot see where to go, how will we get there? If we do not understand what God is saying to us, how can we obey him? My hope is to aid the *seeing* and the *understanding* of the gospel so that we might *live* it more obediently, and through our obedience change a lost and dying world.

CULTURAL WORLDVIEW BLINDERS

Part of the problem is that our vision is clouded by the culture we are immersed in. From the time of our birth, we are surrounded by a cultural worldview that teaches us how to see and understand how the world works. Our worldview gives us a set of glasses to see through; no one can escape its perspective-shaping power. From infancy, our minds absorb what happens around us and we learn how to understand and interpret events. We learn words and language, cause-and-effect relationships, cultural values and how to relate to others. All of this forms a cognitive framework through which we actively engage the world around us. It would be impossible to interact with the outside world without this framework because we wouldn't have any functional way to interpret what we see and experience.

The tricky thing about worldviews, however, is that they are virtually invisible to us. We don't consciously think about them. Our worldview allows us to think about other things, but it rarely appears in our conscious horizon, where we can evaluate it objectively. My worldview is like my contact lenses. They help me to see the world around me, even though I sometimes forget that I have them in. I don't spend my day looking at my contact lenses themselves. I see *through* them. We see and understand our world *through* our worldview. Because we don't consciously think about our worldview, we tend to be oblivious to how it affects and shapes our thinking and perceptions.

Take, for instance, how words and language work. Most of us identify that white stuff that falls from the sky during wintertime as "snow." But an Eskimo sees something very different when looking at that white stuff we call snow. Depending on how you count, they actually have up to fifteen different words for *snow*.* Their worldview and experience have created a way of seeing snow that is richer than our way.

Sometimes, without our realizing it, our worldview limits what we see and understand. It might focus on some aspects and realities of life while totally missing others. Imagine that you are riding in a huge airplane and someone next to you asks, "Where is the landing gear?" You might look around inside the plane or peer through those dinky little oval windows, but you will not be able to see the landing gear. In fact, you probably never even wondered about the landing gear. It is just not something people think about when riding on a plane.

Yet once questions are raised, we realize how limited our perspective really is. The only way to see the landing gear is to get a perspective of the plane *from the outside*. The same goes for our worldview framework. Unless we get an outside view looking in, we will be blind to how our worldview shapes our vision and understanding.

Consider what happens when we enter another culture. By living in that culture for a while, we start seeing our own culture in a different

---

*You can read more about Eskimo words for *snow* at the following website: <www.princeton. edu/~browning/snow.html>.

light. We begin to understand why we tend to act in certain ways and why we value certain things.

When I went to Japan for six months in high school, I realized for the first time just how informal and egalitarian American culture really is. In the United States, it is not uncommon to refer to older people by their first name and to relate to them as peers. The senior pastor of my church is in his fifties, yet I normally call him David. In Japan I faced the difficulty of adjusting my speech to fit the degree of respect expected toward my elders. To call my teacher or pastor by his first name would be a horrible breach of conduct, communicating disrespect and causing me embarrassment. Hierarchy is deeply ingrained and highly valued in Japanese culture. My American values of informality and egalitarian relationships just did not fit. My time in Japan gave me new eyes to see my own culture that I had become used to as I grew up in the States.

AMERICAN INDIVIDUALISM

One of the hallmarks of Western society is the value it places on the individual. The heroes of our culture are people who step out on their own and refuse to conform to society. They are *individuals,* and they venture out in radical individuality. In the movie *Titanic,* the hero and heroine are people who don't let society force them into its mold. They seek to live life to the fullest, no matter what society tells them to do. In the movie *First Knight,* the hero is a poor country boy who rises above his station in life by fighting his way to the top, becoming a noble knight who wins the love of a beautiful princess. Despite how shameful this would be in a culture with a rigid social hierarchy, this appeals to our cultural sentiment for individuality.

The United States Declaration of Independence states, "We hold these Truths to be self-evident, that all Men are created equal, that they are endowed by their Creator with certain unalienable Rights, that among these are Life, Liberty and the Pursuit of Happiness." Today this translates into a zealous pursuit of personal success and enjoyment.

Anything that gets in the way of that pursuit is seen as a violation of our God-given rights.

The benefits of this mentality for individuals are clear. We are devoted to protecting the individual's rights. We affirm the hard work of individuals to pursue their dreams. We recoil at the idea of an individual's rights being trampled. Our legal system is built around the protection of individuals' rights. Clearly there is something good here.

Our particular way of valuing the individual, however, can be so exaggerated that the individual is all we see. This aspect of our worldview limits our ability to see clearly. As a boy, I was once told to insert my name in John 3:16 in place of the word *world*. So John 3:16 says to me, "For God so loved *Allen* that he gave his only Son, so that if *Allen* believes in him *Allen* may not perish but have eternal life." While this wonderfully expresses God's love for me, it distorts the true focus of the verse. God didn't send Jesus to save just me. He sent Jesus to save the whole world. In our focus on the individual, our cultural worldview clouds aspects of reality.

Consider the description of our spiritual armor in Ephesians 6. I was taught to interpret and apply that passage individually. *I* need to put on the helmet of salvation or the breastplate of righteousness. *I* need to wield the sword of the Spirit, the Word of God. I, I, I. I've even seen toy armor made for children to teach them about putting on spiritual armor. Never was I taught to consider that this was a letter written to *communities* of faith, not simply to a solitary individual. Paul is not telling one person how to fight the spiritual battle. He is telling communities how to fight the spiritual battle *together*, teaching them to live out their lives together with salvation on their minds, with righteousness (or justice) firmly embedded in their community life and with a strong commitment to the Word of God. The armor is meant to be embraced by a community in their life together. Yet when we read Ephesians 6, we probably think only about how it applies to us individually rather than what it means for our community of faith.

We call this *individualism*. Individualism is a cognitive framework that sees only the individual at the center of everything. Decisions are made to serve one's individual needs. The purpose of life is interpreted as promoting the lives of individuals. Dreams and aspirations that help individuals get ahead are nurtured. I choose a church or campus fellowship based on what it will do for *my* needs. I read Scripture for what God will say to *me* for *my* life. I do not ask how these will help me to better serve the community of faith for a lifetime. Individual needs are primary.

Unfortunately, I believe that our Western individualism has caused us to misperceive and misunderstand the gospel in a way that blunts the gospel's world-transforming force. Furthermore, the tradition of the Western church, steeped in this individualism, has stamped its approval on narrow conceptions of the gospel that leave us living in ways that do little to change the society around us. Like my childhood rendition of John 3:16, our conceptions of the gospel have been infected by individualism. Where the gospel is supposed to explode into our world with transforming power, it has been co-opted by aspects of our culture so that it blinds us into a quiet cultural conformity.

So is God out to change the world? Yes! But we've been blinded by our culture. And behind the culture, I suspect, stands the god of this age (2 Corinthians 4:4),* who is at work to blind us to the full power and meaning of a revolutionary gospel message. Isn't it time to clear away the clutter that has accumulated around our eyes, refocus our vision and embrace anew the life-transforming message of the gospel?

THE TASK AHEAD OF US

We must do our best to hear the good news of the gospel all over again. We must reexamine the Scriptures and hear the gospel the way the early church heard it. We need to ask questions like, "If we were to ask the

---

*This particular passage speaks of Satan blinding the minds of unbelievers—but can he not also blind the minds of believers?

writers of the New Testament what the gospel was, what would they tell us? What would people like Matthew, Mark or Luke say? How would they react to our rendition of the gospel message?"

Now before you get too nervous, know that I am not going to deny the death of Jesus for sins or the need for faith in Jesus for salvation. I am not going to say anything heretical. I am not going to claim some extrabiblical "new gospel" or "new revelation." Instead, I want to go back into the Scriptures and look again at what they are telling us about the gospel and its implications for our lives.

What I find there is that the gospel is all about the kingdom of God. What is the kingdom of God about? Well, that's for the rest of the book. I also have found many ways in which individualistic assumptions have crept into my faith and distorted my perception of the gospel, which has had significant implications for my life. I have come to understand why Christians and the Christian church are not living out the world-changing dynamic of the gospel, a gospel about the kingdom of God. My hope is that in the next few chapters, I will begin the process of clearing the fog and pointing the way to the good news of what God has done, is doing and will one day finish in his plan to change the world.

PART ONE

THE GOSPEL
OF THE KINGDOM

2

THE GOSPEL?

It was a plastic glove with different colors for each finger. It was my "good news glove," and it accompanied a small comic book that explained the gospel. I've long since forgotten exactly what the book said and what colors the fingers of the glove were. I don't even remember how old I was when I used it. What I do remember is that I wrote my name in the comic book to accept Christ; there was a written prayer at the end of the comic book and I signed my name to indicate that I prayed that prayer. In fact, my family had several of the comic books lying around the house, so I went around signing every one I could find, just to make sure.

I learned at an early age that Jesus had come to die for my sins so that I might be forgiven and have eternal life. I put my faith in Jesus and what he had done for me on the cross; I placed my hope in him as my way to heaven. I knew the gospel pretty well and even learned ways to share it with non-Christians. In college I learned a version of the Navigators' bridge diagram, which visually illustrates the gospel message in a way that helped me to share it with my friends. It was simple: We are separated from God by our sins. The cost of our sins is death. Only Jesus provides the "bridge" to cross over the separation so that we can be with God. We have to admit our sinfulness, believe in Jesus and surrender our lives to him; only then can we walk across the bridge of Jesus Christ to be with God forever. This gospel message is encapsulated in other presentations as well: Campus Crusade's Four Spiritual Laws, the Roman Road (which walks you through verses in the book of Romans) and InterVarsity's First Steps to God all communicate the gospel message in simple, easy-to-understand ways.

But is this the gospel as the New Testament writers understood the gospel? As I studied the Bible and considered the help of various biblical scholars, a new vision of the gospel message began to emerge before my eyes. I had what some people refer to as an "aha! moment." All of a sudden, bits and pieces of the Christian life started to fit together in a more cohesive way. Previously held tensions now fit nicely together into a seamless fabric of consistency. New horizons opened up in front of me as I looked out with new vision at all that God was calling me to. It was as if God had set a new pair of glasses on my nose to correct my severe myopia. Since that time, I have continued to marvel at all that God helps me to see as I look through my "gospel glasses" to read my Bible and consider my life as a follower of Jesus.

The word *gospel,* which means "good news," appears often in the New Testament. Jesus talks about it. We have four narratives of Jesus that we call *Gospels.* Paul brings the gospel to the Gentiles and outlines its implications for his churches in his letters to them. But have we really stopped to consider what Jesus and the New Testament writers *meant* when they talked about the gospel? That might sound funny to you, but think about it for a moment. I found that as I read the New Testament, whenever the writers talked about the gospel I simply read into that word what I *already knew* to be the gospel. Rather than letting Jesus and the New Testament writers tell me what the gospel was, I let my preconceived notions of the gospel dictate its meaning.

But when I tried to start over and let the New Testament speak, I found God opening my eyes to see the gospel anew. Yes, it is about Jesus' dying on the cross for our sins. Yes, it is about our gaining eternal life with God forever. Yet the good news is so much bigger than the limiting box I had been holding it in for so long.

One place where I found this to be true was in the Synoptic Gospels, the Gospels of Matthew, Mark and Luke.* Mark begins his Gospel by saying, "The beginning of the *gospel* about Jesus Christ, the Son of God" (NIV, emphasis added). Now, here is where I expect Mark to begin to help us understand the gospel about Jesus that we all know so well:

- We are all sinners who have rebelled against God.

- Our sins must be paid for in order for us to be with God, but we are unable to pay for them.

- Jesus has come to die on the cross to pay for our sins so that we might be reconciled to God.

- All who believe in Jesus and what he has done for us on the cross can have eternal life in heaven.

This understanding of the gospel revolves around Jesus' substitutionary death for us. So in Mark's Gospel I expect to find Jesus talking about the need for our sins to be paid for. When Jesus talks about himself, I expect him to focus on his role as the One who will pay that price for us: "Here I am! I have come to pay the price for sin that has been hanging over your head for centuries."

But is that what Mark proceeds to tell us? Actually, Mark says surprisingly little along these lines.

Or consider Peter's sermon in Acts 2. The Holy Spirit has just been poured out at Pentecost and the believers have been speaking in different languages of the wonders of God. As a result, all of the people are wondering what is going on. So Peter stands up to explain. Again, I expect Peter to tell the people the good news. I expect him to explain the need

---

*Synoptic Gospels are so named because of their literary relationship to each other. *Syn* means "together" and *optic* refers to "seeing" or "perception."

for our sins to be atoned for. I expect him to excitedly declare that this is exactly what has happened in Jesus. But is this what Peter talks about?

In both cases, I find Mark and Peter to be severely lacking. They just don't seem to do a good enough job of explaining the gospel!

Mark clearly talks about Jesus dying on the cross, but he talks about Jesus dying *for us* in only two places! In Mark 10:45, Jesus says he has come to give his life as "a ransom for many." In Mark 14:22-25, at the Last Supper, Jesus tells his disciples that his blood "is poured out for many." Throughout Mark's narrative, I find little that helps me clearly understand that Jesus has come to die *for my sins.* Why doesn't Jesus spend more time explaining the need for our sins to be paid for? Why doesn't Jesus talk more about his purpose—to die for our sins?* After all, this is the gospel, isn't it? It seems that I would have a hard time helping a non-Christian understand the gospel by using the Gospel of Mark!

In fact, as you look through Matthew and Luke you will find this disconcerting reality again. Only in Jesus' Last Supper statements do Matthew and Luke help us to understand that Jesus has come to shed his blood for the forgiveness of sins. Why isn't Jesus' death for sins more clearly spelled out throughout these Gospels? After all, they are called *Gospels,* aren't they?

In Acts 2, Peter stands up to explain what is happening as the Holy Spirit empowers Jesus' disciples to speak in different languages. What a wonderful opportunity to share the gospel! Yet what does Peter talk about? He talks about how God has fulfilled the prophecies of Joel; he talks about how the Jesus who was crucified was declared by God at his resurrection to be Lord and Christ. And he challenges his listeners to believe in this Jesus for the forgiveness of sins and to receive the Holy Spirit. He implores them to save themselves from a crooked generation. Where is the clear explanation of the "death for sin"? Where is

---

*In the Synoptic Gospels Jesus begins to tell his disciples that he is heading to Jerusalem to die and then to be raised, but he does not explicitly explain *why* he is to die; he does not explicitly tell his disciples that he is going to die for the world's sins.

the invitation to go to heaven by believing in Jesus? Again, I would have a hard time helping a non-Christian understand the gospel from this apostle's sermon.

Isn't it strange that Matthew, Mark and Luke do not give us a clearer explanation of the gospel? Could it be that we are missing something? Could it be that Matthew, Mark and Luke *were* trying to tell us the gospel? Could it be that because we have preconceived notions about what the gospel is, we have missed what they were trying to tell us?

So what *were* they trying to tell us? What did they understand to be the gospel of Jesus Christ? To comprehend this, we must reexamine these Gospels and try to find the dominant themes that manifest themselves in the development of the plot of Jesus' life, death and resurrection. We must pay attention to the message Jesus proclaimed and how that message played out in his public ministry. We must study how these writers crafted their narratives to tell us what was so important about Jesus' coming.

In Mark, when Jesus starts his public ministry he proclaims, "The time is fulfilled, and the kingdom of God has come near; repent, and believe in the good news" (1:15). What was Jesus announcing? What does it mean that the kingdom of God has come near? What was so good about this news? The Greek word translated as "good news" here is the same word translated elsewhere as "gospel," so for Jesus this announcement about the kingdom of God seems to be at the heart of the gospel.

In fact, when we consider Jesus' public teaching we find that the kingdom of God was central to his ministry. Jesus used parables as his primary means of public teaching, and most of them are about the kingdom of God. For instance, he compares the kingdom of God to the following:

- a mustard seed (Matthew 13:31-32; Mark 4:30-32; Luke 13:18-19)

- yeast mixed into flour (Matthew 13:33; Luke 13:20-21)

- treasure hidden in a field (Matthew 13:44)

- a pearl of great price (Matthew 13:45-46)

- a net gathering both good and bad fish (Matthew 13:47-50)

- laborers in a vineyard (Matthew 20:1-16)

- a banquet to which poor and broken people are invited because the rich and upstanding all turned down the invitation (Matthew 22:1-14; Luke 14:15-24)

- a wedding where the bridegroom arrives right when some foolish bridesmaids have left to buy lamp oil (Matthew 25:1-13)

- money entrusted to servants (Matthew 25:14-30; Luke 19:11-27)

The kingdom is also central to Jesus' teaching in the Sermon on the Mount (Matthew 5—7). He assures us that the kingdom is for the poor in spirit and those persecuted for the sake of righteousness. He tells us to seek first God's kingdom and to pray for it to come.

After Jesus was raised from the dead, during the final days of his time on earth, Luke tells us that he went around teaching about the kingdom of God. The kingdom of God was clearly central to Jesus!

We Christians talk about the kingdom all the time, but many of us don't have a clear sense of what it really is. We often hear the phrase "kingdom of God" invoked in worship songs and conversations around the Christian community. But what exactly is the kingdom of God about? Is the kingdom the people of God, the church? Is it heaven? Is it salvation? We rejoice when people enter it ("Yes! John prayed to receive Christ! He's come into the kingdom!"). We give our statements a sense of importance when we invoke the kingdom ("Let's do this for the kingdom," or "Let's have a kingdom mindset about this"). We regularly pray for the kingdom to come as we say the Lord's Prayer ("Your kingdom come. Your will be done, on earth as it is in heaven"). But do we really know what we are talking about as we say these things?

Many of us do have some vague notion of the meaning of the kingdom of God; otherwise we wouldn't feel so comfortable using it in our conversations with one another. As I hear people use "the kingdom" in sentences, I get the impression that they have varying definitions. Sometimes they are talking about the community of faith; other times it's about Jesus' return; and still other times it's tacked onto something to make it sound more important, as in kingdom prayer (not just prayer), or advancing the kingdom (not just dong God's will). I suspect that many are using the word *kingdom* unreflectively.

Yet according to Matthew, Mark and Luke, the kingdom of God was at the heart of Jesus and his ministry. In fact, Jesus himself tells us to seek *first* the kingdom of God. I firmly believe that if we were to ask what the gospel was that Jesus preached, it would have something to do with the kingdom of God.

However, getting a handle on what the kingdom of God is all about from Jesus' teaching and preaching is not easily done. Over and over Jesus explained what the kingdom was like and what it meant to enter it, yet many people just didn't get it. In Acts 1 Jesus' disciples seem confused about the kingdom—even after Jesus' death and resurrection—when they ask him when God will restore the kingdom to Israel. When we, two millennia later, try to wrap our mind around the concept of the kingdom, we face the added obstacle of cultural and historical distance as we seek to hear his message as it would have sounded to the original audience. In many parts of today's world, people are no longer in the habit of talking about kings and kingdoms. Our life experience is far different from that of first-century Jews living under Roman rule.

Even a cursory look at Jesus' teaching about the kingdom presents challenges. Consider the timing of the kingdom. When exactly is the kingdom present? In some verses it seems that the kingdom was present, then and there, as Jesus walked around Palestine. He even declared, "But if it is by the finger of God that I cast out the demons, then the kingdom of God has come to you" (Luke 11:20). In other verses the kingdom seems to be something still to come in the future. In the parables of the

virgins and of the talents in Matthew 25, Jesus talks about what the kingdom *will be like* in the *future,* when he, the Son of Man, returns to judge
the living and the dead. And when Jesus teaches us how to pray, he
speaks of the kingdom as if it is not yet here: "Your kingdom come. Your
will be done, on earth as it is in heaven" (Matthew 6:10). So is the kingdom here now or still to come in the future? Or is it somehow a little of
both?

We dare not let such difficulties drive us into resignation. We dare not
give up trying to understand the meaning of the kingdom of God. We
have to remember that the message of the kingdom was very important
to Jesus. It would be sad if we, followers of Jesus today, failed to grasp
what was so important to him.

CONCLUSION

For many of us, the message of the gospel has been so ingrained that we
never question it. And when we read our Bibles, we rarely stop to exam-
ine whether our understanding of the gospel lines up with what the Bible
says. Our traditions and worldviews have shaped our understanding so
definitively that we rarely stop to reexamine what the Bible says about
the message of the gospel of Jesus Christ. Yet when we reexamine the
Synoptic Gospels of Matthew, Mark and Luke with fresh eyes, a curious
truth emerges: The gospel message focuses less on Jesus' substitutionary
death for us and more on the kingdom of God (not that these two ideas
are mutually exclusive). While it is clearly true that Jesus died on the
cross for us so that we might have forgiveness of sins, the overriding
theme of Jesus' preaching and the central motif in the Gospels is that the
kingdom of God has arrived. But what is the kingdom of God about?

3

THE MESSAGE
OF THE KINGDOM

Jesus arrives on the scene proclaiming, "The time is fulfilled, and the kingdom of God has come near; repent, and believe in the good news" (Mark 1:15). And everywhere he goes he talks about the kingdom of God: how one enters the kingdom, where the kingdom is, what the kingdom is like, what the kingdom will be like in the last day, how God will take the kingdom away from some and give it to others, and instructions to seek and pray for the kingdom.

But what *is* the kingdom of God? What is it about? What is Jesus trying to tell us?

We use the term "kingdom of God" all the time, but do we really know what it means? Is it a place? Is it about salvation? Is it heaven? Is it the church?

Historically, there's been much debate in New Testament studies about the kingdom of God. Most scholars agree that it has to do with God's reign breaking into history and into our world in a decisive and new way to bring restoration to God's lost creation. The kingdom of God is not so much a place, like the United States; or a group of people, like the church; or a distant, future heaven. George Eldon Ladd says that "the primary meaning of the Hebrew word *malkuth* in the Old Testament and the Greek word *basileia* in the New Testament is the rank, authority and sovereignty exercised by a king."[1] He continues by saying that "the Kingdom of God is also the realm in which God's Reign may be experienced."[2] So as I understand it, the kingdom of God is about *the dynamic of God's kingship being applied.*

In the Old Testament we find prophetic hopes that pointed to a time when God would intervene and bring restoration to his people Israel and to his fallen creation. It was about people being reconciled to God, people being at peace with each other, all of the created order of plants and animals existing in harmony, wars ceasing and governments submitting to the divine kingship of God. Isaiah 2 talks about the last days, when many peoples will come to the house of the LORD to learn his ways; God will sit as judge between the nations and they all will beat their swords into plowshares because there is no more war. In Isaiah 11 we read that

> the wolf shall live with the lamb,
>> the leopard shall lie down with the kid,
> the calf and the lion and the fatling together,
>> and a little child shall lead them.
> The nursing child shall play over the hole of the asp,
>> and the weaned child shall put its hand on the adder's den.
> They will not hurt or destroy
>> on all my holy mountain;
> for the earth will be full of the knowledge of the LORD
>> as the waters cover the sea.* (vv. 6, 8-9)

From Old Testament expectations, we get a sense that the kingdom of God was about God's great restoration, the reinstatement of God's intentions for his entire creation. It was God's kingship being applied in a world that had gone awry.

---

*See also Isaiah 61, Jeremiah 31, Daniel 7 and 12, Joel 2, and Micah 4. David Wenham's *The Parables of Jesus* (Downers Grove, Ill.: InterVarsity Press, 1989) has a particularly helpful introductory chapter on the kingdom of God.

An image in C. S. Lewis's *The Lion, the Witch and the Wardrobe* powerfully illustrates this concept. Four children stumble into a magical land called Narnia. The true king of the land is Aslan, a magnificent lion, the Christ figure. Yet at the time of the story, Narnia is under the rule of the White Witch, who has cursed the land so that it is perpetually in a bitter cold winter with no Christmas. But at one point in the story, Christmas *does* come as Father Christmas comes, dispensing gifts. Then springtime begins to invade the bitter winter of the White Witch's reign. The snow begins to melt, the trees release their snow covers, flowers bloom and birds chirp. What is going on? Father Christmas explains, "Aslan is on the move! The Witch's magic is weakening!" We come to understand that wherever Aslan draws near, springtime breaks out in the midst of the bitter winter of the White Witch.[3]

This is what the kingdom of God is about. God's reign descends in and through Jesus and is applied in a world that is not yet fully under his authority. Sicknesses are healed, demons are banished, sins are forgiven and people are assured of God's love for them. Wherever God's kingdom comes, his kingship is applied and the evil of darkness is banished.

The idea of God's kingship being applied in our world, in time and space, was what the Jewish people were waiting for. *This* was what was brought to mind when the term "kingdom of God" was used. And this is what they heard when Jesus came on the scene proclaiming, "The time is fulfilled, and the kingdom of God has come near; repent, and believe in the good news."

In Jesus, we see the kingdom touch down in first-century Palestine. We see him going around proclaiming, teaching about and embodying the kingly reign of God that was breaking into the world. New Testament scholar N. T. Wright states, "God was now unveiling his age-old plan, bringing his sovereignty to bear on Israel and the world as he had always intended, bringing justice and mercy to Israel and the world. And he was doing so, apparently, through Jesus."[4] A new day had dawned; God's reign had broken into our world. God had finally intervened in the person of Jesus to restore his intentions for all of creation. Wherever Jesus draws near, it is there that the springtime of God's peace breaks the bitter winter of Satan's evil dominion. The Gospel writers recognized that a new day had dawned once Jesus came on the scene. A new reality had broken into the present and was growing.

I remember watching the old Errol Flynn version of *Robin Hood*. Good King Richard is off fighting the war, so the land is under the rule of wicked Prince John. Corruption and injustice are rampant. The cries of the poor and oppressed are unheeded by Prince John and his officials. So Robin and his merry men spend their time robbing from the rich and giving to the poor. One day, an entourage of men come traveling through Sherwood Forest. Robin and his men swoop down on the traveling party and begin to relieve them of their worldly goods. The man who seems to be leading the party steps forward and begins to pull off his outer cloak and hood. Behold, atop his head is a crown, and his chest is emblazoned with the coat of arms of King Richard! Good King Richard has returned! Robin and his men quickly fall to their knees. "Sire, we did not know!" At this point of the story, we all know that the end of Prince John's wicked reign is imminent. Soon justice will return to the land. The yoke of oppression on the poor will be lifted; the corruption of court officials will finally come to an end. The good king has returned!

Isn't that much like what happened with Jesus? The King of kings had come to his world. Jesus declared,

The Spirit of the Lord is upon me,
    because he has anointed me
        to bring good news to the poor.
He has sent me to proclaim release to the captives
    and recovery of sight to the blind,
        to let the oppressed go free,
to proclaim the year of the Lord's favor. (Luke 4:18-19)

The end of the reign of sin, death and evil was pronounced in Jesus as he came announcing the kingdom. Behold, the kingdom of God is near. Repent and believe the good news!

LIBERATION

But the kingdom did not come, at least not in all its promised glory. Whereas King Richard returned and took back his throne, Jesus did not—at least not completely. To this day Satan and his forces continue to wreak havoc on God's good creation. We are still waiting for Jesus to fully reign. We are still waiting for Satan to be sent into the great abyss and for all evil to be destroyed. Rather than a coronation, Jesus went to a crucifixion. Rather than being exalted, Jesus was exposed to shame, suffering and death. How does this all fit in with the gospel of the kingdom that Jesus was proclaiming?

Jesus' contemporaries were expecting the kingdom to come with power. Furthermore, their vision of the coming kingdom was of the liberation of Israel from pagan oppressors. We know how God liberated Israel from Egyptian oppressors as Moses led them through the Red Sea and into the Promised Land. For the Jews in the first century, the exodus was one of the primary models of how they expected God's kingdom to come in power. God would come and rescue them from their oppression under the Romans. Although kingdom expectations were diverse among the Jews, they were all looking for some sort of exodus-like event to bring them the blessings of the promised kingdom.[5] They had no idea that the exodus only pointed to something greater, something more complete.

What becomes clear is that the kingdom that Jesus was inaugurating went deeper than a physical and military liberation, and wider than the nation of Israel. God set out to rescue all of creation from sin, death and Satan. He acted to fix all that had gone wrong with his creation due to humanity's sin and rebellion.

When Adam and Eve sinned against God, the sin of humanity had to be dealt with. Throughout Old Testament history God's established means of dealing with humanity's sin was sacrifice.* So Jesus came as "the Lamb of God who takes away the sin of the world" (John 1:29). He died as the ultimate sacrifice for our sins. This message is especially strong in Paul's letters, the basis of so much of our understanding of justification and salvation.

However, when understood in the context of the good news of the kingdom of God, it becomes clear that Jesus' death was not just to get individuals to heaven. It was to fix *an entire creation that had been distorted with the Fall*. When Adam and Eve sinned, everything about God's created order was put in bondage (Romans 8:19-21). It was not just that our relationship with God was broken; *everything* was broken! The life-giving relationship with God that we were supposed to have was severed. The deep, meaningful relationships we were supposed to have with one another were infected with selfishness and pride. And the entire created order was sent off-balance, no longer to operate in its God-given harmony.

The good news of the kingdom of God is that God came to fix it *all*— our relationship with God, our relationships with each other and the harmony of the created order. So Jesus died not simply so that lost individuals could go to heaven but so that all of creation would be redeemed! God really is out to change the world!

The Jews were expecting that the kingdom would come in power to free them from the Romans, but Jesus came in weakness and died the death of a criminal in order that all of creation would be freed from the dominion of sin, death and Satan. The punishment for humanity's sin was poured out on Jesus. He was the sacrifice that paid the debt and took away the punishment we deserve. In Colossians 1 Paul talks about God reconciling an entire creation—everything. Because of Christ's death, all of God's good creation will be restored to its God-ordained glory. This, indeed, is good news.

---

*A variety of sacrifices existed. Not all were about dealing with sin, but it's clear that key sacrifice practices existed to deal with people's sins.

CONCLUSION

So what is the gospel? According to the Synoptic Gospels, the good news of Jesus Christ is primarily that Jesus has come to inaugurate the kingdom of God, to establish God's good reign over all of creation. In the same way that Aslan drew near and brought springtime into the bitter winter of Narnia, Jesus has drawn near to bring the springtime of his redemption into the bitter winter of our fallen world. He died to pay the price for our rebellion and to free creation from Satan's dominion. He will return one day to bring it all to completion and fully establish the kingdom of God. This is good news. This is the gospel!

4

THE GOSPEL OF THE KINGDOM IN OUR LIVES

"Gee . . . look at all those ants."

Andy was staring down at an anthill watching all the ants scurry around. In the background he could hear people yelling things about the ball game. Andy, who was, well, not the best ball player, was out in right field waiting for the end of the half-inning. We all know that when little boys play baseball, no one ever hits any balls out to right field. So Andy had gotten used to looking around at whatever would catch his fancy. This time, it was the ants down by his feet. But the yelling in the background seemed to be getting louder. What was that? It sounded like his name: "Andy! Andy!"

"Whaaaat? Oh, no! Someone hit the ball out to right field!"

When our focus on the gospel is too narrow, we lose sight of the bigger picture and don't realize that God is at work all around us to establish his kingdom. We need to look up, understand the bigger picture and get in the game!

Individualism has narrowed our conception of the gospel to be solely about individuals finding their reconciliation with God, about *my* getting right with God so that *I* can get to heaven. And our mission in the world is to help other individuals find their reconciliation with God.

Although the gospel of the kingdom is certainly about individuals getting right with God, it's also about God's restoration of the *entire creation!* N. T. Wright says the following of the Jewish expectation of the kingdom:

> They were not thinking about how to secure themselves a place in heaven after they died. The phrase "kingdom of heaven," which we find frequently in Matthew's Gospel where the others have "kingdom of God," does not refer to a place, called "heaven," where God's people will go after death. It refers to the rule of heaven, that is, of God, being brought to bear in the present world. Thy kingdom come, said Jesus, thy will be done, *on earth as in heaven.* Jesus' contemporaries knew that the creator God intended to bring justice and peace to his world here and now.[1]

When Jesus came to bring the kingdom, everything that God had made was within the scope of what he came to change. The Old Testament looked forward to the coming of the kingdom as a creation-wide intervention where God would come and make right all that had gone wrong. Sicknesses would be healed, sins would be forgiven, enmity would be eradicated and the created order would be put at peace. The hoped-for intervention of the kingdom of God was expected to touch every aspect of our existence on this earth.

God is out to affect everything! He really *is* out to change the entire world! Jesus came on the scene to announce God's work of restoration over all of his creation. To be faithful to the gospel, we must play our part in the restoration of all of God's creation. Look up! Look around! God is moving to change everything. He is out to change you, inside and out. He is out to change your school. He is out to change your place of employment. He is out to change your community and nation. He is out to change the world!

Notice, too, that the gospel tells us that we are in an unfinished story. History is moving toward a grand finale, and we, as followers of Jesus, are still in the middle of it. The good news is that our good King has already secured the end for us. The sin of humanity that brought us all under the dominion of Satan has been dealt with on the cross. And now we are moving toward the fulfillment of God's purposes.

History is moving. Are you in the game?

SEEKING THE KINGDOM

So what does all of this mean for us? How are we to respond to the good news of the kingdom? Consider what the message of the kingdom means for us as we "seek first the kingdom of God."

Allegiance. The imagery of kingship highlights the call to allegiance. To live under the reign of a king requires people to relinquish any allegiance they might have to another king. As the children in *The Lion, the Witch and the Wardrobe* discovered, it was impossible for them to give their allegiance to both the White Witch and Aslan: it was one or the other. When King Richard returned, it would have been impossible for his people to serve both Prince John and him: it had to be one or the other.

So too, as we consider the call we've received to follow Jesus, we must evaluate whether we serve alternative kings. Are we in relationships in which the other person is more important to us than Jesus? Are we so committed to our dreams and ambitions that we will not let Jesus give us *his* dreams and ambitions for us? Are we so dependent on our financial resources that we will not let God's heart for the poor open our hands in generosity?

The individualism of our culture has convinced many followers of Jesus that he will help us through every struggle and provide for our every need as we pursue our dreams. It's as if Jesus came to serve our needs; in reality, *we* are to serve *him.* Students often come to college all set with a vision for their lives—they imagine lucrative careers and upper middle class lifestyles. They've decided before their first year that they are going to be doctors or lawyers or whatever. So when they relate to Jesus, rather than coming with empty hands for him to fill with his dreams for them, they come with their hands full of their own dreams and say, "Jesus, please bless me as I go after my dreams."

I remember meeting with George (not his real name), a freshman who told me that he had come to faith right before college. He started appearing at some of our fellowship meetings, so I got together with him. I challenged him to consider making a plan to grow as a follower of Jesus. But George said that he just didn't have the time. He was immersed in his pursuit of his dreams to be a wealthy, well-connected businessman after graduation. Still a freshman, he had already made professional business cards to give to his contacts. He held several campus leadership positions and was already involved in community organizations that would pad his résumé. As I talked with him, I asked him, "If Jesus asked you to give up some of your campus activities in order that you could get to know him better and learn how to serve him effectively, would you give them up?" George replied, "Honestly, no. But then again, I don't think he is asking that, so I'm fine." I felt some of what Jesus must have felt when the rich young ruler refused to give away his money and come follow him. Like Jesus, I sadly watched George walk away into a life that crowded out the One who loved him and died for him.

So the gospel of the kingdom calls for our allegiance to God over any other allegiance we might feel compelled to live for. It's about putting Jesus on the top of our life priority list. It's about letting go of anything that will keep us from following Jesus wholeheartedly. It's about getting our vision straight. We are here to serve Jesus and to have *his* dreams for our life, not the other way around.

Integration. To integrate is to bring together into a unified whole that which has been held separate. In terms of living for the kingdom of God, it means that *every area of life* is to be brought together and submitted to the loving kingship of God. Doing that means allowing Jesus into every nook and cranny of our life.

We hear this sort of challenge often enough, but we may not really think about how it is supposed to erase the lines that divide our life into segments. We tend to categorize life into the "spiritual" or "religious," and the "secular" or "neutral." I've heard this called the "sacred-secular split." Often, the effect of this split is that Christian discipleship focuses primarily on the spiritual or religious or sacred areas of life. We're challenged to grow in prayer and Bible study. We're encouraged to get involved in ministry activities at church or in our campus fellowship. We're called to reach out in evangelism. But in the secular or neutral areas of life, which include things like academic classes and jobs, there is less conscious thought about how to live out the kingdom of God. The result is Christians who believe they are following Jesus because they are faithful to daily quiet times, church or campus fellowship involvement, and evangelism. However, they tend to approach the secular areas of life just like anyone else does.

In my work among students, I often find students who get so excited about Jesus that they fill up their time with activities in the campus fellowship. They are active in small group Bible studies, they faithfully attend weekly chapter meetings for worship and teaching, and they are active in sharing their faith with their friends. Yet when it comes to their academics, they skip classes just like other students, they cut corners in their academic projects, and they engage the material in classes not to learn more about God's world but simply to get a good grade. In fact, I remember one student who was so excited about Jesus that she almost flunked out of school. She got so involved in the Christian fellowship that she neglected her studies to the point of academic probation. That all changed when we talked about what it means to follow Jesus in and through academic life. She later went on to be a decent student *and* an active leader in our campus ministry.

Where are the Christian students who are actively seeking to live out God's reign *as students?* In academics, every subject is somehow connected to the divine Author and Creator who made it all possible. Wheaton College history professor and author Mark Noll says the following of the life of the mind in the academic endeavor:

For a Christian, the mind is important because God is important. Who, after all, made the world of nature and then made possible the development of sciences through which we find out more about nature? Who formed the universe of human interactions and so provided the raw material of politics, economics, sociology, and history? Who is the source of harmony, form, and narrative patterns and so lies behind all artistic and literary possibilities? Who created the human mind in such a way that it could grasp the realities of nature, of human interactions, of beauty, and so made possible the theories on such matters by philosophers and psychologists? Who, moment by moment, sustains the natural world, the world of human interactions, and the harmonies of existence? Who, moment by moment, maintains the connections between what is in our minds and what is in the world beyond our minds? The answer in every case is the same: God did it, and God does it.[2]

Noll claims that exercising the life of the mind is important because God matters. In contrast to the utilitarian venture to get good grades simply to get a good job, the very act of studying acknowledges the Creator. Jim Sire, in his book *Discipleship of the Mind*, states, "Scholarship is an act of worship, for it is an unveiling of meaning—an illuminating of what is near and dear to God Himself."[3] As Noll tells us, ultimately learning matters because God matters. Yet Christian students often live out their academic lives as if God does *not* matter. This reflects the sacred-secular split in student life.

As a student, after I had committed my life to Jesus I was very active in campus ministry. I participated in meetings, led a small group Bible study and sought to follow Jesus as best I could. Yet I had no qualms about cutting a class or two when I thought I could get away with it. When it came to my studies, my primary goal was to get the grade. Rarely did I engage in study with an attitude of understanding God's creation. Sadly, I find that many Christian students today look like I did when I was a student.

So much of the university is built around an implicit naturalism that operates as if God is irrelevant to academia. He is not perceived as being relevant to the content of study or to the manner in which one approaches study. If God is ever considered in study, it is as an *object* of study rather than as the source and sustainer by which study is even possible. Often, Christian students simply conform to this way of thinking. They come to the university to devote their time and energy to academic learning, yet they carelessly conduct their academic lives with little thought as to God's reign over it.

Yet the challenge is to integrate one's faith in Jesus into academic life. Jenn, a Northwestern journalism student, talks about her pursuit of balance between faith and intellectual inquiry:

> In a Russian literature course I pored over Dostoyevsky, whose characters in *The Brothers Karamazov* contemplate the existence of God as they suffer the consequences of their misdeeds. In history classes I've seen how Christianity has evolved, for better or for worse, over the centuries.
>
> Even in religion classes, I've grappled with Hegel, who couldn't give me satisfactory answers to life's philosophical questions quite like the Bible could. And although I may never find myself in a science classroom before graduation (I'm a journalist, go figure), friends report to me that they often see God as they study microorganisms whose complex intricacies point to the hand of a divine Creator.
>
> Both in and out of Northwestern's classrooms, God has aided me in developing an all-encompassing faith that I believe will last long past my college years.[4]

I see the pattern of separating the sacred from the secular continue as these students graduate and contemplate what job to take. It seems that it doesn't matter what job they choose, as long as the job is legal and earns a decent income. Usually, the job with the highest salary wins out. Many never stop to evaluate whether the job they take will help or hinder God's kingdom agenda in our world. Or they do not stop and submit their choices to the evaluation of Christian mentors who might help lend perspective as to which jobs might offer opportunities for kingdom growth. The unspoken priorities for many Christians are to make sure that they keep up daily quiet times and find a decent church to belong to. The secular realm of career choice remains a neutral matter. The sacred-secular split remains unchecked.

When people are in their jobs, they may clock into Christian living when they read their Bibles or when they attend a church service or ministry meeting. While they are on the clock at work, however, they do not consciously live out the gospel of God's kingdom reign in and through the job. Other than possibly sharing one's faith with a coworker, Christians on the job often neglect the conscious practice of seeking God's kingdom in and through their daily activities in the office. Men and women who follow Christ must consciously obey Jesus' command to seek first the kingdom of God in the jobs that occupy so many of their waking hours.

Some of us are in positions of authority and influence. Are we using that authority and influence to bring the peace and justice of God's reign over what we are responsible for? I do know of businesses that exude the integrity and compassion that mark the goodness of God. Business executive Joel Gross explains how he views his role in the corporate world:

> As a Christian, if you see that business is a way to serve people, you're going to bring a whole new attitude. You're not there just to enhance yourself, but you're there to raise up the people around you, to bring them along, to put some value into their lives. . . . It's just a completely different perspective. The same with what you do through your customers, your vendors, and through your employees. And then there are also the opportunities to give back to the community, too. That's the kind of leadership that the Christian in business can have.[5]

Some of us aren't in positions with a great deal of influence, yet are we doing what is in our power to bring tastes of God's goodness where life is bitter with sin and injustice? Do we consciously think through how our actions and relationships at work reflect the goodness and justice of our King? Are we working in a way that shows our commitment to live for Jesus in all things? Are we engaging in projects in a way that God would delight in?

So the gospel of the kingdom of God means that if we are to follow Jesus, we are called to consciously live out his reign in every area of life. There is no sacred-secular split under God's kingship. We must live out the gospel in our classes and jobs, not just in the Bible studies we attend, the worship services we participate in and the personal devotions we engage in. It is all a matter of *integration*.

Mission. Furthermore, when it comes to living out the gospel in our world, we are called into a holistic mission to our world. When I graduated from college, I felt God's call on my life to pursue missions. So I committed myself to help reach people with the gospel wherever God would have me go. So for me, missions was all about reaching people and helping them find saving faith in Jesus Christ. I think that most Christians today, when talking about being sent out in mission to our world, have a similar image. Like me, they picture a person going to some exotic place, possibly living in a grass hut and bringing the gospel to that place. We all build our call to mission on the Great Commission in Matthew 28, to go and make disciples of all nations.

In my pursuit of a life in missions, I enrolled in the missions program at Wheaton Graduate School. As part of my coursework, I remember struggling through the issue of how social action fits into missions. What place does feeding the poor and working for the cause of the oppressed have in our work for the gospel? To reach out in love to people means that we cannot overlook people's physical needs for the sake of their spiritual needs. But it also sounds awfully underhanded to feed the poor and care for the oppressed *so that* they might become Christians. So what is the balance? And what takes precedence if one is forced to choose between serving physical needs or sharing a verbal presentation of the gospel?

Today this tension is all around us. When faced with a world that is full of poverty, corruption and injustice, where do we invest our efforts? In my campus ministry we have felt God's strong hand on us to pursue racial reconciliation. Yet for some this sounds like either a concession to the multicultural agenda of the university's political correctness or a diversion from the real work of the gospel, which is to save lost college students. Most believe that there are some essentials when it comes to reaching out with the gospel in our world: evangelism, discipleship and missions. Therefore, feeding the poor or dealing with racism becomes an "elective" for those who are "called" to such agendas.

Yet if the gospel is about God's reign breaking into our world, what does that mean for our relationship with this world? If the good news that Jesus proclaimed was that God was beginning to reclaim a lost creation and restore it to his creational intentions, does it not call us to live for and seek the love, truth and justice of God in *whatever way it is being challenged in our world?* Yes, we are to seek the salvation of men and women of all nations. No, that does not necessarily take precedence over feeding the poor, seeking justice for the oppressed or dismantling racism and corruption in society. As we individuals interact with our world, we need to consider how God's reign would be seen in all of our encounters and relationships. As a church, we need to consider the community around us and seek its welfare as a way of fleshing out the kingdom of God.

Neil Shorthouse helped to found Communities in School, America's largest community-based organization that helps children succeed in school and prepares them for the rest of their lives. He views his work as his mission:

> I have a responsibility to leave this world the very best that I can, better than the way that I found it. . . . For right now . . . it is trying to affect the institution of education. . . . We've got kids that have problems with gangs, we've got kids that have problems with health issues, we've got kids with family problems, we've got kids with incarceration issues. . . . I need to be asking God to use me in a very specific day-to-day routine of

writing proposals, meeting with people and discussing strategies. Yester-
day, we had twenty-five to thirty people talk about, "How are we as a state
going to stop these children from dropping out of school—how do we
prevent that?" That, to me, is a pretty important Christian thing to do, and
I bet a lot of people in that room were Christians. Now they weren't wav-
ing a Jesus banner while they were doing it, but we were working on putting stuff on flip charts and ideas and so forth, which to me, I think, came
out of God's Spirit in them to help find a way for us to be what we are
supposed to be and do what we are supposed to do for these children who
are trapped in the institutions that we, as human beings, have created.[6]

ALLEGIANCE, INTEGRATION, MISSION (AIM)

Like little Andy out in right field, we may need to lift up our head and
look around. The gospel of Jesus Christ is about a wholesale, complete
renewal of the entire created order. God came into our world, in Jesus
Christ, to reclaim all of his creation, to fix what had gone wrong when
humanity sinned. The gospel has gotten . . . well . . . *bigger* in its implications on how we live. Not only are we called to devotion in our "religious" activities like Bible study, prayer and evangelism, but we are also
called to integrate God's reign into every aspect of our existence.

Take proper AIM as you consider what it means to follow Jesus and
live out the gospel. Is your allegiance fully devoted to Jesus? Are you in-
tegrating his kingship into every area of life? Are you seeking to live out
God's mission to restore his lost creation?

PART TWO

LIVING IN THE TENSION OF THE KINGDOM

5

WHERE'S THE KINGDOM?

"God, where are you?!"

I was watching my wife crumble before my eyes. She was balled up in a fetal position, desperation in her eyes. She was sobbing, her whole body shaking from the anguish. She had been the victim of incest and repeated sexual abuse in her family. For much of her adult life she had bottled up the pain and anguish of her childhood and adolescence, and had sealed it under a firm lid. But now that lid had popped off and the agony had exploded with a devastating fury. In dealing with it all, days stretched into weeks, then months . . . then years.

God, where are you? I put on the best face I could as I interacted with the world around me. Most of the time I appeared calm and composed. But on the inside I was falling apart. Some of the hardest times were in corporate worship when the congregation would sing of victory and peace in the Lord—a victory and peace my wife and I were clearly *not* experiencing.

What's more, deep inside I felt like I had gotten ripped off. For whatever reason, I had soaked in a conviction that entering the kingdom meant fulfillment and protection from pain. Sure, I knew there would be hard times, but I thought that walking with Jesus meant that I had a leg up on the rest of the world, that the hard times wouldn't hit me so hard because I had him on my side. Implicitly, I had worked out a deal with God: *I believe in you and serve you, God, and you just help me have a happy marriage.* But now hard times had hit, and I felt no sense of God softening the blow. It had bashed my wife and me from behind and left us battered and bleeding on the ground.

Life as a Christian isn't always so wonderful. All the high and lofty talk about the peace of God or victory over sin often sounds hollow. I look at my own life and the lives of people around me, and the Christian message doesn't seem to line up with what we are experiencing. Christian friends work hard to mend an ailing marriage, only to fail and walk their separate ways. Persistent and ugly sins seem so intractably locked on my soul despite all my prayers for God's strength and transformation. The church, the body of Christ, often feels like a battleground of gossip, political intrigue and hypocrisy.

Where's the kingdom, Jesus?

Then there's ministry. How many times have I gone to some conference or heard of some church where incredible miracles are taking place? I hear about hundreds of people becoming Christians, churches growing from thirty to three thousand, people getting healed of their crippling diseases and entire cities rocking from the powerful work of God in a local church. Then I go home to my campus ministry or my church, which seem rather bland in comparison. So I try to apply in my ministries what these other ministries have done—perhaps a different approach to evangelism or prayer, or a new way to set up small groups. Many of these ministries promise the rest of us that if only we do what they do we will see the same sort of "success" in ministry. Yet no matter how well I seem to apply their lessons and principles, I never seem to see the same results. So I plod along on campus with my fellowship and at my church, seeking to be faithful to the ministry God has called me to. All the while I have this hollow feeling in my chest: *Is it me? Did I do something wrong? Maybe I'm just not a good leader? Or maybe it's the people . . . that's it! It's other people who just can't seem to get it together. Maybe it's the pastor.* On and on it goes as I wonder why I am not seeing the fruit of ministry that seems to come so easily for others.

Where's the kingdom, Jesus?

The gospel is the good news that in Jesus, God came to assert his kingly reign over his lost creation. Sicknesses are to be healed, evil banished, injustice eradicated and forgiveness for our sins pronounced. All of creation is to come under the kingly rule of its Creator. Wonderful. So where is it? What happened? That was two thousand years ago! Did the kingdom really come? Did God really enter into our world to restore his broken creation? Or was Jesus mistaken? Or maybe God's just slow.

You see the problem. The good news of the kingdom was about a wholesale renewal and restoration of the entire created order—humanity reconciled to its Creator, people and nations at peace, the created order in God-ordained harmony. Isaiah pointed to a time when creation will be in harmony as the wolf lies down with the lamb and children play at the cobra's nest (Isaiah 11). He speaks of the end of wars as swords are turned into plowshares (Isaiah 2). He promises that the Lord will wipe away every tear (Isaiah 25).

Yet we look around us today and are quickly reminded that the kingdom has definitely not come. All you have to do is wake up in the morning and read the newspaper. Wars continue, a missing child is found buried in a field, a husband and wife divorce, French fries are linked to cancer, a teenager fires an automatic gun into a high school cafeteria—such incidents seem to be a daily occurrence.

What's more, it does not seem to get much better for the follower of Jesus. Pain, suffering and injustice rip into our lives with the same apparent randomness as in the lives of non-Christians. And many times, it assaults us so forcefully that it makes us wonder where God is. Other times, we get disillusioned by how mundane God's work seems to be in our churches and fellowships.

The New Testament shows us that it wasn't much different for Jesus' first followers. After Jesus died and was raised from the dead, it was not as if the kingdom had come in all its glory. People still got sick, people still died, and poor people still went hungry. All was not well in the world. So where was the kingdom? Had it come or not?

THE AGE TO COME

As the Jews thought about the kingdom of God, they broke up history into two grand eras (see figure 1). There was the Old Age, which was characterized by sin, death and evil, and the Age to Come, which was characterized by God's life, peace, justice and love. The kingdom of God was another way of talking about the Age to Come. An aspect of the Jewish hope was that at some point in time, God would send his Anointed One to inaugurate the Age to Come, putting an end to the Old Age and all of its misery.* Evil and the evildoer would be judged, and the faithful would be ushered into the blessedness of the Age to Come. No more sin, no more death, no more evil.

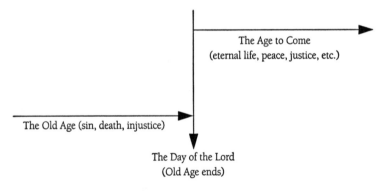

Figure 1. Two grand eras of history

---

*In fact, I would argue that the biblical mandates against the "flesh" and for the "spirit" are more about these two ages rather than about the "physical" and "spiritual." I don't think the biblical writers like Paul were saying that the physical was bad while the nonphysical or spiritual was good. That was the error of the Gnostics that the church condemned as heretical. No, the idea is that we are not to live according to the Old Age but instead in the new age of the kingdom of God.

So when Jesus arrived on the scene proclaiming the kingdom, his listeners were looking to see whether Jesus would bring in the Age to Come.

The confusing thing was that in some ways, the Age to Come did seem like it was breaking in as Jesus healed sicknesses, cast out demons and raised dead people to life again. He even announced, "The time is fulfilled, and the kingdom of God has come near; repent, and believe in the good news." Yet in other ways, it didn't seem as if Jesus was bringing in the Age to Come at all. The ambiguity was such that John the Baptist sent messengers to ask, "Are you the one who is to come, or are we to wait for another?" (Matthew 11:3). John had just been imprisoned by a cruel puppet king (Herod), the Romans were still in power, the people of God were still living under oppression and Jesus wasn't really doing anything about it. I'm sure John was wondering what was with this Jesus. As New Testament scholar George Eldon Ladd writes, "How could He [Jesus] be the bearer of the Kingdom while sin and sinful institutions remained unpunished?"[1] Yet in response to John, Jesus replied, "Go and tell John what you hear and see: the blind receive their sight, the lame walk, the lepers are cleansed, the deaf hear, the dead are raised, and the poor have good news brought to them. And blessed is anyone who takes no offense at me" (Matthew 11:4-6). His response was as if to say, "Yes, I am the One. Look at the signs of what God is doing."

IS IT HERE, OR ISN'T IT?

Furthermore, when Jesus talked about the kingdom, it wasn't altogether clear whether it was really present or still to come. At some points, Jesus talked as if it was close at hand and present in their midst. For example, he says in Luke 11:20, "But if it is by the finger of God that I cast out the demons, then the kingdom of God has come to you." And in Luke 17:20-21 he says, "The kingdom of God is not coming with things that can be observed; nor will they say, 'Look, here it is!' or 'There it is!' For, in fact, the kingdom of God is among you." Jesus claimed that the kingdom of God was right there, in his ministry, in their midst.

At other times Jesus refers to the kingdom of God as if it will come in the future. In Matthew 24 he says the Son of Man will come in glory at a time people aren't expecting him, and he calls his disciples to faithfulness until that time. In Matthew 25 Jesus explains that *at that time the kingdom of heaven will be like* the parable of ten virgins waiting to meet the bridegroom; or the parable of talents, in which the master entrusts his money to his three servants while he goes away; or the parable of the sheep and the goats, which describes an ultimate parting of the ways between the faithful and unfaithful. The parables all refer to a future time when Jesus will return in glory.

So which is it? Is the kingdom of God here, or is it still to come in the future?

JESUS' DEATH

To confuse matters even more, Jesus died on a cross! A crucified king was definitely *not* an expectation of those looking forward to the kingdom of God and the Age to Come. As Christians, we have the benefit of hindsight and can look back on passages like Isaiah 53 and see visions of a crucified Messiah. But prior to Jesus, there was absolutely *no* expectation that the Anointed One, the One who would bring in the kingdom, would die. And Jesus did not just die—he was executed as a treasonous criminal. As Paul wrote in 1 Corinthians, the idea of a crucified Messiah was a stumbling block to Jews.

During Jesus' day, there were numerous uprisings led by revolutionaries who claimed, in one way or another, to be establishing God's kingdom.[2] Some of them, like Jesus, were known for claiming to be God's Anointed, the Messiah. All of them failed, and one common element of their failure was that the Romans crucified them. The Romans developed this cruel form of punishment for the worst criminals and for enemies of the state. Part of the horror of crucifixion was the public statement it made. As people saw convicts dying on their crosses, they understood what awaited anyone who had thoughts of rebelling against the Roman

Empire. And, more significant for us, crucifixion marked the utter failure of the one consigned to die on the cross. Their pretensions to messiahship and their attempts to foment revolution for the kingdom of God were soundly denounced by their public death and humiliation.

Jesus' death on the cross could mean nothing else but that he had failed and that his claims to be sent by God were a lie. He seemed to be no more than another Messiah wannabe in a long line of others who had failed and were executed by the Romans. For followers and skeptics alike, there was just no way that Jesus was something more . . . at least, that's what they would have thought.

THE RESURRECTION

Yet we know that Jesus was raised from death to new life. It's hard for us to realize just what an unprecedented, incredible shock this was for Jesus' first followers. Apart from his own words about being raised from the dead, his disciples had absolutely no hints that this would happen. Nothing in the Old Testament pointed to a resurrected Messiah (other than brief clues that we can see now only in hindsight).

What's more, the meaning of Jesus' resurrection is often lost on us since we don't understand the Jewish expectations for the Age to Come. One key aspect of the Age to Come, the glorious new age of the kingdom of God, was that the faithful would be resurrected. You hear this in Martha's reply to Jesus after he told her that Lazarus would rise again: "I know that he will rise again in the resurrection on the last day" (John 11:24). The idea was that when God stepped into history to bring the Age to Come, all the faithful who had died would rise up to enjoy the blessings of the kingdom of God. Resurrection was not part of the Old Age, where sin, death and evil still reigned. It was clearly a part of the Age to Come, when God would reign in glory and his peace and justice would permeate his world.

So when Jesus was raised from the dead, imagine what those early Jewish disciples thought. "It's here—the Age to Come has begun! Jesus has risen from the dead!" Right before their eyes, they were seeing the beginnings of the resurrection that marked the Age to Come. The future was right before them, saying, "Touch my hands and feel my side . . . I'm really here . . . I'm really alive."

They would have wondered, "But where are the resurrected heroes of faith from the Old Testament, like Abraham and Deborah? Where are my uncle, Jacob, and my grandma, Miriam?" The odd thing at Jesus' resurrection was that it was only Jesus who was raised from the dead. The more general resurrection did not happen. Again, this continues the confusing pattern: the Age to Come did seem to arrive in Jesus, yet in some very clear ways it did not arrive. So what was going on?

THE HOLY SPIRIT

Then there was the whole business of the Holy Spirit. In Ezekiel 36:26-27, God spoke about the Age to Come: "A new heart I will give you, and a new spirit I will put within you; and I will remove from your body the heart of stone and give you a heart of flesh. I will put my spirit within you, and make you follow my statutes and be careful to observe my ordinances." And in Joel, God pointed to the Age to Come when he said, "Then afterward I will pour out my spirit on all flesh; your sons and your daughters shall prophesy, your old men shall dream dreams, and your young men shall see visions. Even on the male and female slaves, in those days, I will pour out my spirit" (2:28-29). These passages and others like them show us that, in addition to the resurrection of God's people, another key sign of the Age to Come was the pouring out of God's Holy Spirit on his people.

Then *bam!* Pentecost happened! The Holy Spirit was poured out on the early church with a loud sound like that of a violent rushing wind, and something that looked like tongues of fire came to rest upon each of them. Empowered by this Spirit, they all rose up and began to speak about Jesus in different languages to the crowd of Jews gathered in Jerusalem for Pentecost, Jews who had traveled from many nations to worship at the temple. Peter then stood up to explain that all of this was a sign that the long-awaited Age to Come had arrived! And throughout the book of Acts, it is clear that the Holy Spirit had come and was powerfully at work within the church to empower God's people for witness to the entire world.

All right! The Age to Come had arrived! The promised Holy Spirit had been poured out on God's people just as God had promised. But wait. Wars and violence continued, all people were definitely not at peace, and key members of God's people were being killed! Where were the promised peace and justice of the kingdom of God? Once again, the curious reality was that, while the Age to Come was clearly manifested in the coming of the Holy Spirit, it was not *fully* seen in all of its glory as anticipated by the Old Testament prophecies.

So as we look at what happened in Jesus' day, we are left with this puzzling truth. In some meaningful respects, the kingdom of God and the Age to Come *did* arrive. The Jews were expecting the resurrection of the faithful in the Age to Come, and here was Jesus raised from the dead. God's people looked forward to the coming of the Holy Spirit at the Age to Come, and God powerfully poured out his Spirit at Pentecost. Yet it was incomplete. It was expected that all the faithful would be resurrected, but it was only Jesus who was resurrected. The Age to Come promised peace, justice and a restored creation, but wars, injustice and conflict continued despite the coming of the Holy Spirit on God's people. So had the promised Age to Come, the kingdom of God, come or not?

6

THE TENSION

As a little boy, I just could not wait for Christmas to come. As soon as that first present materialized under the tree, I'd eagerly await the day when I could storm into our living room and tear the wrapping paper off all my presents. My sister and I would even pull out our family's department store catalogs and circle all of the toys we were hoping for. I wanted Christmas Day to come so badly that I could not sleep on Christmas Eve. Come midnight, I'd go to my mom and ask whether I could open my presents because it was officially Christmas Day. Mom would always say, "Go to bed! You can't open your presents until *after* you've slept through the night!" I even remember one Christmas when I woke up at about three o'clock in the morning. Realizing that I'd actually slept a little and woken up on Christmas Day, I woke up my sister (despite the darkness), headed to the living room and started to open my presents.

Now imagine waking up one Christmas Day as a little child and being told that you could open only two presents, and all the rest would have to wait until the next week!

On a much grander scale, isn't that what it must have been like for the early disciples? The people of God had been waiting and waiting for the kingdom of God and the Age to Come. Then with Jesus, it all looked like it was about to happen. Instead, the kingdom of God seemed to come incompletely.

So had the kingdom of God arrived in Jesus or not? The answer seems to be both "yes" and "no." Prior to the full, triumphant arrival of the kingdom, aspects of the future Age to Come had reached back into the present and touched down right in the midst of the Old Age of sin, evil and death. Nestled firmly in the soil of this evil age were real bastions of glory that had invaded the Old Age in the person and work of Jesus. New Testament scholar George Eldon Ladd talks about this as the "presence of the future." The Age to Come had really begun, but the Old Age had not ended as expected.

D-DAY

In World War II, on that fateful day now called D-Day, the Allied forces stormed the beaches of Normandy in the war against the Nazis. Left and right, soldiers of the Allied army were being picked off and killed. Yet at great cost, they finally secured the beachhead. And once that happened, Allied victory against the Nazis was practically assured. The war was all but over. All that was left was to mop up enemy forces and push for complete surrender.

Jesus' work on the cross was the like the D-Day victory in the war against Satan, sin and death. It secured the victory; it was the decisive battle of the war, but it was not the end of the war. The end of the war will come when Jesus returns for a second time at the end of history to bring his revolution to completion and fully establish the kingdom of God. That will be V-Day, the Victory Day of the war.[1]

So the new reality of the kingdom really had arrived in Jesus. While it had not arrived in all its fullness, the decisive battle securing final victory had been won. As Jesus declared "It is finished" from the cross, the D-Day victory of the kingdom was irrevocably secured.

That's why Paul, on the one hand, declares that complete victory and salvation have been accomplished in Jesus Christ:

So if anyone is in Christ, there is a new creation: everything old has passed away; see, everything has become new! (2 Corinthians 5:17)

[God] raised us up with him and seated us with him in the heavenly places in Christ Jesus. (Ephesians 2:6)

Through [Christ] God was pleased to reconcile to himself all things, whether on earth or in heaven, by making peace through the blood of his cross. (Colossians 1:20)

And on the other hand, Paul still talks about the coming day when the victory and salvation will be complete:

I consider that the sufferings of this present time are not worth comparing with the glory about to be revealed to us. For the creation waits with eager longing for the revealing of the children of God; for the creation was subjected to futility, not of its own will but by the will of the one who subjected it, in hope that the creation itself will be set free from its bondage to decay and will obtain the freedom of the glory of the children of God. (Romans 8:18-21)

But our citizenship is in heaven, and it is from there that we are expecting a Savior, the Lord Jesus Christ. He will transform the body of our humiliation that it may be conformed to the body of his glory, by the power that also enables him to make all things subject to himself. (Philippians 3:20-21)

For the Lord himself, with a cry of command, with the archangel's call and with the sound of God's trumpet, will descend from heaven, and the dead in Christ will rise first. Then we who are alive, who are left, will be caught up in the clouds together with them to meet the Lord in the air; and so we will be with the Lord forever. (1 Thessalonians 4:16-17)

So we live on after the D-Day of the cross but still wait for the final V-Day, when the trumpets will blow and Jesus will return in glory to establish God's good reign forever over all of creation. The kingdom has come in a very decisive way, yet it is still to come in all of its glory. So we pray, "Your Kingdom come. Your will be done, on earth as it is in heaven."

THE RESURRECTION

Paul explained that Jesus' resurrection was the first one of many and represents the assurance that others will follow: "For as all die in Adam, so all will be made alive in Christ. But each in his own order: Christ the first fruits, then at his coming those who belong to Christ" (1 Corinthians 15:22-23).

As a small boy at school, I remember my teacher giving each student in my class a small seed to plant in a little cup of soil. We kept them near the window in the sunlight and watered them every day. I remember that my name, Allen, was taped to the front of the cup so I knew which one was mine. At first, I wondered what the big deal was. Nothing was happening. I was just pouring water on dirt. So what? But wonder of wonders, a small sprout pushed its little head through the soil to greet me. Then my excitement grew. Each morning I'd rush to my plant near the window to find more of my little sprout friend emerging from the soil. So I would eagerly give it its daily feeding of water. Before too long, I had a sizable plant in full bloom.

Jesus' resurrection is sort of like the little sprout head that greeted me that fateful morning. It wasn't the final product. It wasn't the complete plant in full bloom. It was simply the "first fruit" of what was to come. As the "first fruit," Jesus' resurrection gives us two assurances.

The first is *the inevitability of the coming harvest.* Once I saw that little sprout poke its head through the soil, I knew that the fully blooming plant was on its way. In the same way, as we look on the resurrection of Jesus, we are assured of our resurrection that is still to come.

We may grow weary and disillusioned in waiting for the kingdom to come. But we must look to the resurrection of Jesus as a banner planted firmly in the ground of history, assuring us that our redemption is on its way. It's a wonderful landmark in the long journey of kingdom living that assures us that our future is secured. The little sprout has appeared. Let us patiently wait for the coming trumpet call when the dead will rise up to greet their King!

The second assurance is a *glimpse into our future.* Jesus is the first resurrection to happen. In seeing his resurrection, we see a glimpse of our
own resurrection. The little sprout gave me a glimpse of what was to
come. And what was to come was good.

For many of us, our vision of the life to come is of a light and disembodied sort of existence flying around in the clouds. We are taught that
our "souls" shed our "physical" bodies as we fly away into glory. Our
"physical" bodies are necessary but sinful encasings for the real person,
the "soul." So heaven and the kingdom of God are about leaving these
bodies behind.

Yet according to the Scriptures, the future body we will receive is seen
in the resurrected body of our Lord Jesus: "Just as we have borne the image of the man of dust [Adam], we will also bear the image of the man
of heaven [Jesus]" (1 Corinthians 15:49). Paul speaks of our future bodies as *transformed,* not disembodied.* He says that we will put on the
"imperishable" (1 Corinthians 15:42). It's not that we will shed our body
and fly off as disembodied spirits. No, we will be given an imperishable
body. The state of our body in our resurrection life will be what N. T.
Wright calls "incorruptible physicality."[2]

So to look at the resurrected Jesus is to see our future. He was the first
one to be resurrected. We will one day follow him into our blessed future.

Often I hear Christians argue for the credibility of Christ's historical
bodily resurrection, usually in an attempt to validate the Christian faith.
They argue that if Jesus was truly raised from the dead, this backs up the
Christian claim that Jesus is God, that he is unique among all other reli-

---

*The biblical picture of our future is clearly of an embodied existence. In 1 Corinthians 15:35-
57, Paul talks about the different bodies. We currently have the perishable body but will be
given an imperishable one at the final resurrection. Unfortunately, the English translation of
verses 44-47 appears to contrast the "physical" body with the "spiritual" one (as in the NIV).
This gives us an impression that the old body is the physical one while the resurrected one is
somehow not physical. What is translated "physical" in our English Bibles, however, is really
more like "soulful." The root of the word is *psyche,* which we normally translate "soul." The
issue is what *animates* our bodies. Paul is telling us that our current physical bodies, which are
animated by "soul," will one day be physical bodies animated by "spirit."

gious leaders and that he therefore ought to be listened to as he tells us about life, death and salvation. This is all well and good. Paul, too, tells us that God raised Jesus from the dead with power to show us that Jesus is the Son of God (Romans 1:4).

All of this, however, misses a key teaching of the Scriptures about Jesus' resurrection: that it is both an assurance of our destiny and a glimpse into our future. The Age to Come has really begun in Jesus and we have seen it—we have seen *him*—walking among us. The resurrected Lord Jesus is our living hope. He is the author and pioneer of our faith who has gone before us and will come back to take us to glory.

The good news of the resurrection of Jesus is that the Age to Come has actually arrived and begun. And in this resurrection, we can be assured that the completion of its coming is on its way. Furthermore, we can also see in the resurrected Jesus a glimpse into our wonderful future. Yes, it feels like a long wait—but rest assured, the resurrection of the kingdom of God has already begun! Look at Jesus and see your future. George Eldon Ladd writes, "We are living on the heavenward side of the first stage of the resurrection. This puts a new light on the whole human predicament. Heaven has already begun in that the resurrection has already begun to take place."[3] Jesus' resurrection is one key sign that the kingdom has arrived. Yet we await Jesus' triumphant return, when it will all be brought to consummation.

THE HOLY SPIRIT

In addition to the resurrection of Jesus, the gift of the Holy Spirit is an assurance of the coming kingdom. In Romans 8:23 Paul calls the Holy Spirit, like the resurrection of Jesus, "first fruits" as he encourages us to wait with hope for the future day of glory. Therefore, New Testament scholar Gordon Fee writes, "the Spirit was both the certain evidence that the future had dawned, and the absolute guarantee of its final consummation."[4]

When you make a down payment, you pay a sum of money toward

the purchase of a house or a car as a promise to pay the balance at a later time. A part of what is owed is put forward ahead of time as a pledge to pay off the balance at a future time. Incredibly, God has made a down payment *to us* in giving us the Holy Spirit to live inside us. In 2 Corinthians 1:21-22 and Ephesians 1:14, Paul calls the Holy Spirit a deposit (or down payment) that guarantees what is to come. The Holy Spirit is God's down payment to us to bring the kingdom in all its fullness. So in a sense, the presence of the future kingdom has already been given to us in the Holy Spirit. It is only a partial payment, but it is God's assurance that the rest is on the way.

Therefore, the Holy Spirit is the avenue through which we experience foretastes of the future kingdom of God, when all of creation will be made right. It is by the Spirit in us that we experience intimacy with God. It is by that same Spirit that the power of God is manifest in our lives. Yet all of our experiences of intimacy and power are only glimpses of future glory. Your intimacy with God may fluctuate, but those moments of warm closeness with God are real, tangible experiences of your future, deep, passionate intimacy with God that will never grow cold when you finally get to live in his new creation. When you experience those moments in which God powerfully works in your life in acts of healing or provision for need, you can consider it a testimony to the power that will be unleashed one day when all of creation will be made right and redeemed. All of this is given us by and through the Holy Spirit, who was given to us when we believed and who now dwells in us as we walk in faith.

THE TWO STAGES

When we consider the reality that the resurrection of Jesus and the gift of the Holy Spirit are first fruits of the Age to Come, it makes sense that New Testament scholars talk about the kingdom coming in two stages. The Jews were expecting the kingdom of God to arrive all at once, but what happened in Jesus can be seen in figure 2:

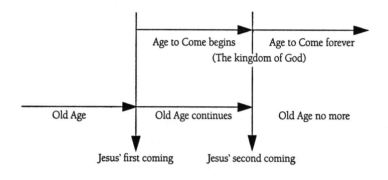

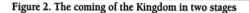

Figure 2. The coming of the Kingdom in two stages

While the kingdom of God did come in Jesus' first coming, it came only in part. The full measure of the kingdom will come at Jesus' second coming. Furthermore, although Jews expected the Old Age to end when the Age to Come arrived, we now see that the Old Age continues and will end only when Jesus returns a second time to fully usher in the kingdom of God. The kingdom comes in part with Jesus' first coming but will come in fullness at Jesus' second coming. It's like D-Day in World War II. D-Day was the decisive battle that assured ultimate victory for the Allies against the Nazis. But V-Day, the victory day of the war, was still to come when the Nazis finally surrendered and signed the peace treaty. In Jesus, the D-Day of the war against sin, Satan and death has been secured for us at the cross so that the Age to Come has begun. But the ultimate V-Day of victory is still on its way and will take place when Jesus returns and the Age to Come arrives in all its fullness.

So we who live between the two comings of Jesus live in the "in-between" times, when the kingdom is "now but not yet." It's here in some ways, but the kingdom will only fully be here when Jesus returns in glory. The resurrection has begun in the sense that the first one has already happened in the person of Jesus. Yet the rest of the resurrection will happen only at the end when Jesus returns and the trumpet blows.

The Holy Spirit has already been given to us, not as a full payment of the kingdom but as a down payment and promise to "pay off the balance" when the kingdom arrives in its fullness at Jesus' return.

So we now live with the tension of what writer Michael Gorman calls the "overlap of the ages."[5] We live in a period where both the Old Age and the Age to Come are happening at the same time. We experience the tension of this overlap all the time. Sometimes the joy of God's kingdom washes over us with such force that we cannot deny his transcendent presence with us. A family member becomes a Christian; worship with God's people is full of the Spirit's power; a friend is miraculously healed of cancer. Yet at other times we struggle with the realities of sin and evil in a fallen world. I selfishly snap at my wife or cut someone off on the freeway; prayers seem to go unanswered while frustration mounts higher and higher; violence increases in the Middle East. The Old Age continues to plague us while the Age to Come fills our life with experiences of transcendence.

This makes sense of so much of the New Testament's teaching. On one hand, the New Testament writers make very bold, definitive statements about what has already happened in Jesus. Paul talks about the already completed side of salvation—we've been justified (Romans 5:1), God has seated Jesus at his right hand and exalted Jesus above every rule and authority (Ephesians 1:20-21), and God has rescued us from the dominion of darkness (Colossians 1:13). Yet in Philippians 3, Paul talks about the incompleteness of his experience. He wants to attain the resurrection of the dead but has not done so. He presses on to take hold of the prize for which God has called him. All over the New Testament, we find the tension of what God has already completed in Christ and what is left incomplete as we, the church, await Jesus' return.

THE TENSION

Understanding this tension is essential to make sense of why we, as followers of Jesus, still face struggles and incompleteness. Entering the kingdom does not mean automatic fulfillment and exemption from pain. It does not mean the struggle with sin will end and holiness will always be easily within our grasp. And it does not mean that all ministry and mission will be "successful"* in efforts to do kingdom work.

Yes, the joy of the Spirit that we sometimes feel is real; yes, we really do experience his love and grace in our lives; and yes, sometimes we do see wonderful things in ministry. But no, we do not experience the *fullness* of that joy, love and grace in all of its wonder. We do not experience the completeness of our victory and redemption . . . at least not yet. As Paul says, "now we see in a mirror, dimly, but then we will see face to face. Now I know only in part; then I will know fully, even as I have been fully known" (1 Corinthians 13:12).

The Christian life is often presented as a pathway to fulfillment or an escape from pain and suffering. I understand where some of that comes from, because it's partially true. On the "now" side of the kingdom (as opposed to the "not yet"), we do find a very real peace with God and comfort for our pain. For some of us, miraculous healings and awesome evidences of the Spirit take place in our life. We really do experience the presence of God right in our midst as we worship and serve him.

But if we stop there and don't recognize the not-yet of the kingdom, we are setting ourselves up for disappointment and disillusionment. The Old Age of sin and death still does smack us in the face sometimes, and we struggle to stay standing. The not-yet of the kingdom helps us understand why our knees buckle and our eyes glaze over at times like those. The kingdom hasn't fully arrived yet. The spiritual battle is deadly, and we must fight the darkness in the certain hope of coming glory.

I found one example of this tension in a New Testament ethics book. In the midst of an academic explanation of the now-but-not-yet tension,

---

*I put *successful* in quotes because it's not always clear what true success in ministry really means. Sometimes, success may mean simply being faithful despite the lack of external signs of success.

New Testament scholar Richard Hays gets personal as he talks about a friend, Gary, who struggled with homosexuality and eventually died of AIDS. Gary could not get around the teaching from the Scriptures that homosexuality is wrong and that it is not God's intention for us. So Gary wrestled with the implications for his own life as he sought to follow Jesus the best that he could. As Hays seeks to explain the implications from the Scriptures, the now-but-not-yet reality of the kingdom plays a key part.

> On the one hand, the transforming power of the Spirit really is present in our midst; the testimonies of those who claim to have been healed and transformed into a heterosexual orientation should be taken seriously. They confess, in the words of the Charles Wesley hymn, that God "breaks the power of cancelled sin; He sets the prisoner free." If we do not continue to live with that hope, we may be hoping for too little from God. On the other hand, the "not yet" looms large; the testimonies of those like Gary who pray and struggle in Christian community and seek healing unsuccessfully for years must be taken with no less seriousness. Perhaps for many the best outcome that is attainable in this time between the times will be a life of disciplined abstinence, free from obsessive lust.[6]

Life is hard. We will continue to face disappointments and to struggle as we walk with Jesus. The Old Age of sin and death is still alive and kicking. It infects everything in us and around us. But one day God will put an end to its destructive invasion.

On the other hand, the kingdom has really come and is present in our midst. The power of the resurrection and the Holy Spirit is at work pushing back the darkness. It is not all disappointment and struggle. Jesus is at work in your life and ministry by the power of the Holy Spirit to bring the springtime of his redemption. It is real when you see and experience the power of God in your life. When Jesus came, died on the cross to free us from sin and poured out the Holy Spirit, the power of the kingdom was unleashed. It has been unleashed in our world. It has been unleashed in your life.

As I consider my own life and the lives of those around me, I think of the difficulties of dealing with the not-yet of the kingdom. When I was younger, the fervor and idealism of the Christian life burned brightly. I think some people got singed from the heat emanating from my excitement. I remember graduating from college with a willingness to go wherever the Lord would lead me, to face any hardship I would encounter and to conquer any evil the Lord would allow into my path. Now that several years have passed, I have experienced some tough ministry battles, seen way too many disappointments in ministry, watched far too many marriages end in divorce and seen the devastating effects of this world's evil in my own life. At times it is tempting to opt out of it all. It becomes tempting to give up the dreams of making a difference for God. The fire that blazed in my youth burns low and flickers for want of more fuel. In the next chapter I will share with you not only how I hang on but also how the flame can burn more brightly.

7

LIVING WITH THE
TENSION

Understanding the dynamic of the kingdom has caused me to reclaim
the Lord's Prayer.

> Our Father in heaven,
> hallowed be your name.
> Your kingdom come.
> Your will be done,
> on earth as it is in heaven.
> Give us this day our daily bread.
> And forgive us our debts,
> as we also have forgiven our debtors.
> And do not bring us to the time of trial,
> but rescue us from the evil one.
> (Matthew 6:9-13)

Earlier, I had grown very tired of the Lord's Prayer. Having been raised
in a church that said it week after week, it just felt like meaningless rit-
ual. After all, I thought, isn't it better to just pray what I feel, to pray what
spontaneously wells up within my heart and mind? Rote prayers
smacked of institutionalism and deadness to me.

But now it makes so much sense to me why in Jesus' model prayer for us, we are instructed to pray, "Your kingdom come. Your will be done, on earth as it is in heaven." While living in the now-but-not-yet period, we are praying for God's power and reign to invade the present. And we are also praying for the kingdom to come in all its fullness one day. The entire prayer, in fact, is an expression of the pray-er's desire to live life according to the kingdom of God. We petition our King for daily provision ("Give us this day our daily bread"), we ask for the forgiveness of God's reign as we seek to live that forgiveness out with others ("And forgive us our debts, as we also have forgiven our debtors"), we ask for the King's leading to keep us from sin and evil ("And do not bring us to the time of trial, but rescue us from the evil one") and we acknowledge God's eternal reign ("For the kingdom and the power and the glory are yours forever").

In Stanley Grenz's book *Prayer: The Cry for the Kingdom,* he writes, "In the Bible, prayer is eschatological*—it is directed toward the kingdom of God. In prayer, the believer beseeches the God of the future with the desire that the marks of God's rule (forgiveness, sustenance, deliverance, and the Spirit's fullness) may be present in the current situation, which is filled with want, need, and insufficiency. Petitionary prayer, in other words, requests the coming of the future into the present."[1] What Grenz recognizes is that biblical prayer is kingdom-focused prayer. As is modeled in the Lord's Prayer that Jesus taught us, prayer is about seeking the kingdom of God.

So now the Lord's Prayer has become a daily affair as part of my devotional life. I not only say it daily, I think through the categories of the Lord's Prayer as a guide to other things that I ought to pray for. What frames my prayer life is the idea of asking God for his kingdom reign to invade my life in every way.

Let us give thanks for the very real presence of the kingdom in our

---

Eschatological refers to something having to do with the end of history.

midst as we experience glimpses of glory. But let us also not lose sight of the incompleteness of that kingdom as we look ahead to its consummation. And in the struggle to live with the incompleteness of that kingdom, let us plead with God to give us more and more glimpses of the Age to Come. As Jesus taught us, let us diligently pray, "Your kingdom come. Your will be done, on earth as it is in heaven."

KINGDOM PERSPECTIVE

Another way in which the tension of the now-but-not-yet has affected my life is that I've let go of the expectation that life with Jesus will be one of complete fulfillment and safety. Yes, there will be days when the wonder of the now of God's kingdom fills my heart with indescribable joy. But there will also be days when the not-yet of the kingdom leaves me with pain, frustration and longing. In those days I try to remember that the kingdom has already come as the beginning of its coming fulfillment. I try to remember that in the resurrection of Jesus and the giving of the Holy Spirit, we've been assured that the kingdom has touched down for real and will come for real one day when Jesus returns. And I beseech my King for more of his kingdom to come into my present day by day.

Furthermore, I ask God to show me where his kingdom is invading our world, and I intentionally look for it. Through the spiritual disciplines of solitude, Bible study and prayer, I put my "kingdom glasses" on and try to find glimpses of the Spirit at work in and around me. Spiritual disciplines are avenues through which kingdom power and perspective can flow into our lives. I've realized that spiritual disciplines are not simply exercises to do to grow in faith; they are "Spirit-ual" disciplines, disciplines in which the very Spirit of God can take deeper hold of my life and give me eyes to see the presence of the very kingdom of God!

One practice that I've learned from my pastor about reading my Bible devotionally is to ask myself, *Why is God bringing this particular passage into my life at this particular time?* Sometimes I read a passage I've read many times before, but God speaks to me in a new way through it because the Spirit connects the meaning of the passage with a specific situation in my life. I first "listen" intently to the passage and ask God to show me the main theme or image in the passage (for example: a truth about God, a truth about me or a challenge for obedience). Then I close my eyes and think through the realities of my life (the key situations I am facing, the key relationships I must consider, or the projects and agendas I have before me). Then I invite the Spirit to take the truth of the passage and connect it with an area of my life. This takes time. One cursory reading of the passage just will not do. I must have a good twenty to thirty minutes of Bible reading and reflection to do this. When I do, God speaks into my life, and his kingship is made real and tangible for me. He gives me new eyes to see my life through the truth of his kingdom reign. Without this, I will miss my King's voice and I will blindly go on my way without eyes to see the kingdom in and around me. Therefore, I must give myself to the spiritual disciplines of Bible study and prayer.

Also, in the midst of the struggles of living in the not-yet realities of my life, the body of Christ often becomes for me the tangible presence and agent of God's kingdom. As I've sought to walk alongside my wife in her pain, God has brought people around us who flesh out the kingdom for us and speak words from the future into the present. Every two weeks I meet with Bert, Ken, Pat, John and Steve. They love me unconditionally. They pray fervently for me. And through it all, I know that they will be there for me. They flesh out the presence of the kingdom for me and remind me that I am not alone. Beyond these men, there are a host of others who have been praying for Diane and me through our hardship. They often send messages of support and encouragement telling me not to lose hope. Furthermore, two men—Dave and John—have met regularly with me, listened to my life's journey at different times and spoken into my life words of encouragement, challenge and insight that I know God has given them to give to me. As I hear God speak to them, my vision gets transformed and I see anew the hope and presence of the kingdom.

And finally, week after week as I go to church, I have the opportunity to see glimmers of the kingdom all around me. God's Word is available as the Scriptures are read and preached. The reminders of God's presence are made available as I come to the Lord's Table. The hope of the kingdom is made plain as we sing praises, say the liturgies and reaffirm our faith together in speaking the creeds. Often, church can become a ritualistic exercise that one is duty bound to perform. Yet with eyes to see and a heart attitude that is looking for the kingdom, church becomes another means by which the invisible kingdom becomes visible.

Sometimes it is hard to see our way through the not-yet of the kingdom. But we must try to take hold of the truth of the present kingdom and see anew the reality all around us. Through spiritual disciplines such as prayer and Bible study, through looking to the community of faith and through the weekly celebration of the Lord's Day with the body of Christ, we must strive to make our way.

THE WAITING

In the tension of the now-but-not-yet, the waiting is the hard part. We must wait with a proper attitude and understanding of the times. In Romans 8:19-22, Paul talks about the waiting on this side of glory.

> For the creation waits with eager longing for the revealing of the children of God; for the creation was subjected to futility, not of its own will but by the will of the one who subjected it, in hope that the creation itself will be set free from its bondage to decay and will obtain the freedom of the glory of the children of God. We know that the whole creation has been groaning in labor pains until now.

Paul says that all of creation is waiting for the revelation of the children of God. Creation is waiting for the day when the kingdom will come at Jesus' return and we all will be raised up to resurrection glory. And we are reminded that all of creation will be made right when the kingdom comes in all its glory. We are reminded that it's about not just individuals getting to heaven but also a whole creation being redeemed by God.

In the meantime, however, creation is groaning for its liberation. We look around at our world and we see the groaning. Our world is groaning in pain. The not-yet of life this side of glory is full of pain and suffering.

Paul compares this groaning of creation to labor pains. I must confess that, as a man, I've never had to give birth to a baby. I've heard, however, that it's painful. OK, *really* painful. But the nature of this particular pain is that of anticipation. This pain is anticipating something wonderful, the birth of a child. Despite how painful it is, the parents are eagerly anticipating what the pain is signaling: their little one is on the way. After the pain and agony, the exhausted mother rests in unspeakable joy as her child sleeps in her arms. All the pain was worth it.*

Now imagine what it would be like for a woman in labor if she does not know she is having a baby. "Oh my! What is happening to me? *Ouch!* That *really* hurts!" Imagine the desperation and horror as the sharp pains attack her insides for no apparent reason. Ridiculous, don't you think?

In talking about creation's groaning, Paul wants us to understand that all of it is not just meaningless pain and agony. No, it is signaling the coming of something wonderful: the blessedness of the kingdom, the beauty of seeing all of creation liberated from its decay and human beings resurrected to glory. As people of the kingdom, we do have to live in a world that is groaning in pain. But we need to know that the pain is not to be forever. The pain is just a prelude to glory. We must hang on.

I wonder whether part of the reason why the church is so silent these days is that we Christians have grown disillusioned. We've been battered and beaten up a little too much in life. For some people, that has been enough to provoke them to walk away. Christianity didn't work. For the rest of us, we continue to live the Christian life, but disappoint-

---

*Anyone reading this who has given birth is probably rolling her eyes at how naive I am about the realities of childbirth, but I hope that does not take away from the point of Paul's instructions.

ment has taken root deep within our souls. We resign ourselves to doing our basic Christian duties—we go to church, read our Bibles and pray our prayers. But we wonder deep inside whether this Christianity is for real. *After all,* we ask ourselves, *why does life have to be so hard? Shouldn't life be easier, especially for those of us who have chosen to walk with Jesus?* So we take on an attitude that we believe is more "realistic" but that is actually more disillusioned.

Underneath the disappointment and disillusionment, however, is the seed of a lie about mistaken expectations. In choosing to follow Jesus, you expected that life would get "better." Part of what "better" meant is that you'd be protected from pain, you'd find victory over your sin, and life would be just that much easier because Jesus was now on your side.

For a while, perhaps, some of that really was taking place. The joys of walking with Jesus were incredible. The victories you were experiencing over sin and temptation were exciting. The undeniable instances of God's intervention were astounding. This just deepened the lie.

But then sins and struggles attacked and didn't seem to go away. Pain and hardship lingered way too long. Deep and intractable sins just wouldn't be thrown off. Loss and tragedy that seemed to have no apparent purpose devastated your world. And disappointment and disillusionment set in. *What happened?* you asked yourself.

The gospel of the kingdom of God is that God's reign has broken into our world. God has come to us in Jesus Christ to reclaim all of his lost creation. But that kingdom has not arrived in all its fullness. Satan and the Old Age of sin and death are still alive and kicking, and they are fighting hard to destroy your faith. Despite the power of the Old Age, however, the power of the kingdom is stronger, and it will one day put an end to the Old Age forever. Christ's resurrection and the pouring out of the Holy Spirit are proof of that. The kingdom is on its way. Even now, that kingdom is at work in you and all around you. So hang on. Don't give up!

All of the agony from my wife's abuse is far from resolved. Relationships seem irreparably broken. My beautiful wife's soul has been damaged in ways I cannot begin to understand. And our vision of God's calling on her life has become completely uncertain. Yet we hang on. This is not the end. One day, Jesus will bestow on my bride the crown of glory and wipe away every tear. And together with her and all the saints, I will be able to bask in the beauty of God's new creation. Even now, we are seeing glimpses of the kingdom and assurances of the Spirit's presence granting us hope to keep going. And so we pray, "Father, your kingdom come. Your will be done, on earth as it is in heaven. Amen."

PART THREE

THE MISSION
OF THE KINGDOM

8

SEEING STARS

An old story tells about a little boy who walked along a beach that was covered with thousands of starfish, all dying in the sun as the tide went back out to sea. The little boy, out of compassion for the starfish, started to throw them back out to sea one at a time. A man came by and said, "It's no use. You'll never make a difference. There are just too many." The boy replied, "It will make a difference for"—he picked up another starfish—"*this* one." And he threw it out to sea.

This story communicates the significance of making a difference in someone's life, no matter how small it might seem in the grand scheme of things. But isn't it a bit disconcerting? We're left with the feeling that the world's just too big to change. All that really matters is helping that one person in your life right now.

Let's make the picture brighter. Now it's not just one little boy on the shoreline, it's thousands upon thousands—no, wait, two billion—men, women and children. Great! The world of dying starfish is changed! Or is it?

Something is wrong. We reportedly live in a world with two billion Christians. Why isn't the world changing for the better? Something is amiss in the story.

Part of the problem, I suspect, is that there's something wrong in our thinking about *how* we change the world. My guess is that for most churches and Christians, the way we think we will change the world is one person at a time. We go out and share the gospel with people near us at work and in our community, and we support the work of those who are crossing cultural barriers to bring the gospel to other peoples and nations. The idea is to win the lost, one by one by one.

The assumption underneath all of this is that once people become Christians they will effect change in the world around them. Pretty soon, in places where there are enough Christians, those places will be fundamentally changed by the gospel. Simple enough, right?

Well when I look around, it seems to me that something has been lost in the translation. I believe that our presence in the world has lost much of its intended effectiveness because we've lost a vision of the gospel being about the kingdom of God.

We've already discovered that the gospel of Jesus Christ is about the presence and coming of the kingdom of God. We've seen that the gospel is about God coming to us in Jesus Christ to establish his reign over all creation, every nook and cranny. Yet our traditional conceptions of the gospel are much more individualistic, focusing on individuals finding reconciliation with God through the death of Jesus rather than on God's restoration of his entire creation. It's more about people getting "saved" and less about bringing God's will into every aspect of life and society. It's more about helping people escape this earth to get to heaven rather than working to see more of heaven invade this earth. But the gospel is more than the good news that we can be saved; the good news of the kingdom is about creation being restored.

Here is where I believe something got lost in the translation.

Once I heard someone say, "The only reason why God hasn't taken me off to heaven yet is so that I might share the gospel with as many people as possible and take them with me when it's time for me to go." If the gospel is primarily about God's work to bring individuals to himself, then the primary mission for the Christian is to help other individuals find reconciliation with God through Jesus and then train them up to help others find reconciliation with God. This becomes the essential centerpiece of our interaction with the world around us.

But if the gospel is about God coming to establish his reign of justice and peace over all his creation, then our mission as Christians is to see God's will, his kingly reign, happen in and around us wherever that is possible. It's not just about saving souls but about seeing that the poor are fed and the oppressed are freed. It's about caring for the orphans and providing good education for our children. It's about challenging ideologies that counter biblical truth. It's about effecting change in public policy and creating social systems that are more in line with God's intentions for his world. It's about seeing his reign fleshed out wherever we set foot in our world.

I remember going on a night "star hunt" at church camp. Our counselors had hidden neon stars all over the campground. They were tucked away in trees, hidden under stairways, even taped on the backs of some of the adults who were walking around the camp. In cabin teams, our goal was to gather as many of those stars as we could find. So as we dashed around the camp, my mind was racing: "Stars! Find stars! *Stars! Stars! Stars!*" As I ran through the camp, I was oblivious to my surroundings—the incredible array of real stars splayed out in the heavens above me, the eerie cast of the moon on the lake, the sounds of night creatures croaking in the dark. I'd even neglect to say hi to adults as I'd snatch stars off their backs. All I could think of was *"Stars! Stars! Stars!"*

When I think of our individualistic conception of the gospel, I wonder whether we Christians are running around with "stars" in our eyes, oblivious to our surroundings. God has called us to feed the poor, but we just want to save their souls. God wants us to change the social systems that oppress people, but we just want to evangelize them. God wants us to reform business practices to be more equitable for the underprivileged, but we continue to make our profit while we hold evangelistic luncheons for our business partners.

When I was a student I looked for opportunities for evangelism wherever I went. As a fraternity brother, I started an evangelistic Bible study for my brothers. I took on different leadership roles on campus and in my fraternity house. I was a pledge educator for one class of incoming fraternity pledges. I was a counselor for an overnight orientation camp that my college ran for freshmen at the beginning of the year. And one year I was a part of student government as a representative for my fraternity. In all of these avenues of campus involvement, I looked for opportunities to share my faith.

What I did not do was consider how to spread the fragrance of God's kingdom in other ways. As a pledge educator, I did not consider trying to create a pledge-training program that sought to build the character of true brotherhood, scholarship and service in those young men. Instead, I went along with the traditional pledge program that was full of inane activities that sought to demean pledges and teach them our songs and meaningless facts from the fraternity handbook. As a counselor for freshman camp, I did not consider how I could help craft a program that truly cared for the freshmen. Instead, I just did my best to help Christian students find InterVarsity, and I looked for opportunities to share my faith with non-Christians. As a representative on student government, I did not think through ways that I could help the student government bring about positive change on campus that would reflect what God would be pleased with. I just did not think broadly enough of what it meant to seek the kingdom. For me, all that seeking the kingdom of God meant was seeking the conversion of lost friends on campus.

Now, I'm probably oversimplifying the reality and not doing justice to the ways Christians are seeking to love our world and represent Christ with integrity and kindness. However, I suspect that because many Christians think that the most important thing they can do is to help others find salvation in Christ, the Christian church's mission is targeted toward the salvation of lost people. Much less significance is attached to being an agent of the kingdom in and around us in all of our interactions, responsibilities and activities.

When the focus of changing the world becomes fixated on the salvation of lost people, the significance of seeking kingdom change around you in other ways is diminished. You go to work and try to be a good Christian, but in your mind you think that the real world-changing drama is in your witness with your colleagues. No! The real world-changing drama is a day-to-day, minute-by-minute affair of bringing the influence of God's kingdom into all areas of life. It's about loving your neighbor and your enemies. It's about using your influence to bring about kingdom change around you. It's about incarnating the kingdom in that office and banishing the darkness of sin, death and injustice *wherever* that darkness manifests itself!

Joel Gross is the president and CEO of Sticky Business, a company that works on large vehicles and equipment. He explains how he sees his business dealings as a way to love people in Jesus' name:

> Every day there are people issues. And there are needs that people have. And that's opportunity. It's an opportunity to love people. There's opportunities with your vendors—do you pay your bills on time? How do you deal with vendors when you can't, when you get behind? And of course with your customers—do you tell them the truth? Do you tell them the truth when you screw up, when you make mistakes, or do you try to cover up those mistakes? I mean—that's where the opportunity is. . . . It's in the day-to-day interactions of business that your opportunities are to love your neighbor as yourself, and then of course, obviously, to love God. And, you know, we're just stewards, we're the managers [of what] . . . he's given to us; this isn't something I've created, but that he's given to me.[1]

Joel recognizes that *through his business* he can reach out with the love of Jesus. It does not have to be only about evangelistic encounters but also about extending the love of his King through the day-to-day realities of his life in the business world.

The church as a whole needs to wake up and look around! Yes, we need to reach out to lost people who need Jesus. But we also need to consider what God is calling us to in our communities, nation and world. We need to take seriously the need for the kingdom at the societal level in such areas as education, economics and the environment. We need to speak into the world's conflicts and hostilities. We need to be a fragrance of springtime in the bitter winter of our lost world!

Please understand me: I am not denying the need to do evangelism. Not at all! But the gospel of the kingdom demands a more integrated, holistic approach to our interactions with the world. Graham Cray quotes Rene Padilla in stating, "The Gospel is Good News concerning the Kingdom, and the Kingdom is God's rule over the totality of life. *Every human need therefore can be used by the Spirit of God as a beach-head for the manifestation of his kingly power.*"[2] Whenever and wherever we confront the effects of sin, that interaction becomes a place for us to seek and serve the kingdom of God. It's not just about lost souls but also about a lost creation. And the kingdom of God is about a creation restored.

So my concern is that with a more individualistic approach to the gospel and its ministry implications, we shortchange the significance of the mission of the kingdom. We subtly undermine the need for and significance of a holistic approach to life and mission by putting all of our focus on the salvation of lost individuals. And the church may even blind its people to the opportunities they have in their daily interactions to be agents of the kingdom, to be "missionaries of the kingdom." We put the "stars" of evangelism in their eyes and they lose sight of everything else.

In my work with students, I've noticed that Christian students often fall into the trap of thinking that the only mission they have on campus is to witness to their friends. It's my dream that more and more of our students would catch a vision for the kingdom so that they influence every sector of campus life: residence hall advisors who are seeking to transform dormitory life; journalism students who are seeking to transform the campus newspaper; fraternity and sorority students who are seeking to influence the Greek system toward true fraternity and philanthropy;

students who are banding together to think through the Christian perspective on academic research projects. Then seeds of kingdom change could take root and transform the university for years to come.

Furthermore, it's my dream that these same students would then enter the workplace seeking to bring kingdom change there. They would choose jobs that would strategically partner their academic training with careers that will influence society toward justice and truth. They would find ways in the context of their jobs to bring the refreshing breeze of the kingdom into their workplace. They would steward their wonderful resources in a way that would establish beachheads of the kingdom all over our world.

A few weeks ago one of our college students, Liz, went on an urban project and was deeply challenged by what she experienced there. As a result, she said, "For the future, I'm thinking about going into socially responsible business or public interest law. To me, this has been one of the biggest steps of faith CUP [Chicago Urban Plunge] challenged me to take, to start thinking about social justice in terms of how I can use my position of privilege as an upper middle class Asian American to help out those less fortunate than me."

Consider your life in the world. Have you been running around with "stars" in your eyes, possibly overlooking opportunities to see the kingdom fleshed out around you? Consider your church. Are there ways your church needs to reevaluate its calling to be a corporate agent of the kingdom in our world? Does it need to reconsider what it means to have a holistic approach to seeking the kingdom of God? Reconsider your day-to-day life and think through what it might mean for you to seek the King's agenda in your interactions, responsibilities and activities.

To start, try picking one area of your life where you are involved with the world around you. If you are a student, are you involved in student activities or student government? Are you involved in a social group like a fraternity, sorority, dorm floor community or campus club? If you are not in school, are there areas of social or community activity that you are regularly involved with? Is there a project or team at work that you are regularly involved with? Pick one. Then pray and brainstorm. What would this look like in God's kingdom, under God's reign? Where is there truth and life to celebrate? Where is there distortion and short-coming that need to be restored to God-given intentions? Include other Christian friends in your brainstorming session. Then write out ways you can take practical action. What are particular activities, big or small, that you could do to bring about kingdom change? Invite God into all of this and then try doing some of the things you wrote out that could help to bring about kingdom change in that area of your life.

In addition to seeking the salvation of non-Christian friends and co-workers, you are an agent of the kingdom engaged in a world-changing drama every day of your life.

OUR COMMITMENT TO DEAL WITH SOCIAL ISSUES

It is clear that the Christian church has done some wonderful things for the poor and oppressed in the name of Jesus. Many of our missionaries are working to alleviate poverty and suffering. Historically, Christian missions have set up hospitals in places that desperately need medical resources. The church has always worked hard at reaching out in love to those in need.

But how essential is it for every Christian and every church to deal with social issues?

I think that it is already assumed that we are supposed to reach out to lost people with the gospel. (Whether we are really doing that is another matter.) I am confident that in any evangelical church I set foot in, I will find some evidence of a commitment to evangelism and world missions. There might be an "evangelism committee" or regular evangelistic pro-grams or even a pastoral staff person responsible for the evangelism min-istry of the church. And the church will undoubtedly have a missions budget that supports missionaries and missions causes in other parts of the world.

What I am not confident of finding is evidence of a commitment to deal with issues such as poverty, societal inequity and racism. A church might be set right in a city yet do little to deal with the struggles of the underprivileged in their neighborhood. Church members drive in from the suburbs and hear sermons on topics like prayer and evangelism, worship and tithing, yet engage in no programs that help to raise the quality of living for the people living in the neighborhood of their church.

I think of the campus fellowships that I oversee. I'm grateful that we are becoming known for our evangelistic efforts. The campus is realizing that we are on campus to help people find out more about God. We have regular meetings devoted to helping not-yet Christians come and investigate the faith. We have small group Bible discussions where a Christian student helps non-Christian friends deal with their questions about God.

Yet when it comes to responding to issues of racism on campus or poverty in the city, we are not the ones the campus comes to for help. Sadly, the evangelical Christians on campus are not known for their activism in seeking justice for the oppressed, food for the hungry and peace in a world of violence. In fact, the organizations that are regularly sponsoring forums about world peace and organizing projects to feed the hungry are not Christian groups.

One day when we were considering whether we should focus on racial reconciliation, one leader's response was, "I don't want to deny that racial reconciliation is important, but after all, the important thing is that we help people meet Jesus, right?" In his mind, when we need to focus our ministry efforts, it is assumed that we will focus on evangelism over and above other things like racial reconciliation. This expresses the kind of narrow thinking about gospel ministry that I am concerned about.

This should not be! Our gospel proclaims that Jesus came to free creation from the bondage of sin and to bring God's reign into our world. Our gospel tells us that God wants to change every nook and cranny of creation to reflect his goodness, justice and peace. He wants to save lost sinners from hell. He wants to bring peace between enemies and provide dignity for all. He wants to feed the hungry and free the oppressed. He wants to do it all! This is the gospel! How dare we narrow its meaning to individual salvation alone?

How much more effective would our evangelism be if all Christians and all churches were characterized by a commitment to caring for the poor and dealing with social issues that trouble our world? My ministry on campus must deal with a stereotype of Christians—that all we are interested in is saving people's souls. We are not known to be interested in social and political issues. We are not known for getting involved in forums that deal with current social issues that hit the front-page news. We are not the ones out there demonstrating for causes that advocate peace, justice and compassion. But the world needs to see that our faith really does make a difference for life, especially as we deal with some of the most vexing social struggles, like race, gender and class oppression.

When the gospel is narrowed to a message about individual salvation, the mission of the gospel is about saving lost individuals. Yet, as we have seen, the gospel is more than a message about individual salvation; it's a message about God's redemption of his entire creation. Without denigrating the work of evangelism, we need to look around at our world and take stock of places of need. As Padilla said, "Every human need . . . can be used by the Spirit of God as a beach-head for the manifestation of his kingly power."

Westside in Jacksonville, Florida, was once a thriving community. Yet when the Potter's House Christian Fellowship took up residence there in 1991, it had become a poor community with almost no economic trade. Now the community is seeing economic revival, and many credit that to the Potter's House and its pastor, Vaughn McLaughlin. The church has two dozen ministries, many of which help to empower people for better lifestyles. When asked why a church like The Potter's House would build in the midst of a poor community, McLaughlin responds,

We have the ability to repair what is broken, to correct what is wrong. God has graced us to save this place. A local church ought not just drive in on Sunday, have an hour-and-a-half of preaching and singing, and then leave. If you're in the community, then you ought to affect that community.

I ask other pastors, "If your church were to leave the community you're in, what impact would that have? Would they miss you? Would they weep?" I think our community would miss us if we weren't here. I hope they would. We have built relationships with the people of our community and with retailers in hopes of saving this community. That kind of networking can save a community. We are the community.[3]

Look around you. God has put you in situations right now that give you opportunities to seek God's kingdom agenda of peace, justice and reconciliation. Is his kingdom at work? Is it in your neighborhood? What are those opportunities and how might you be able to get more involved? What would it mean for your church to reach out with the love of God to flesh out the kingdom of God?

9

RETHINKING THE MISSION

The start of the game was normal enough. Everyone got their money and rolled the dice to move around the board. Soon, however, I knew I was in trouble. When I passed "Go" I got $50, but when Jenny passed "Go" she got $300. Those were just "the rules of the game," according to the banker. It got worse. I would try to buy property in one color scheme in order to be able to build houses and hotels. But Jenny! As soon as she bought something, the banker offered to sell her a house or hotel! When I asked to do that, the banker firmly replied, "That's not allowed . . . for you." As the game moved along, I was in perpetual fear as I faced the gauntlet of Jenny's hotels littered across the board. Vermont, St. James Place, New York, Illinois, Marvin Gardens . . . all boasting their wealthy hotels! And when Jenny had to go to jail, the banker warmly said to her, "Oh, that was just a mistake. No need to go to jail; just go visit." Unfair! Unfair! Unfair! No matter how hard I worked or how wisely I tried to play the game, it was useless! Now Jenny, feeling sorry for me, started to be easy on me, letting me pay less for landing on her hotels, even loaning me money when I was getting down to my last dollar. Pretty soon, I was flat broke; all my property had been mortgaged off to pay my debts, and my cash was gone. I had nothing.

The game was "Modified Monopoly." It was designed to teach us the harsh realities of our society, in which it is hard for the poor and under-privileged to rise above their poverty. It was meant to reflect the sad truth that resources and wealth are more accessible for the upper and middle class and nearly impossible for the poor to attain. It left indelible marks on us who played.

So what are we to do when the deck is stacked so badly against the poor? In the game, often the rich would start to feel guilty, so they would try to be generous. They would start giving money away or forgiving debts that were outstanding. Rarely, however, would anyone ask about the rules. It was just "the way the game was played." Players did their best, whether with generosity or with greed, to play within the frame-work of the rules.

This highlights a blindness that hampers us in our attempts to bring kingdom change to our world. In the story of the boy and the dying star-fish, the boy sought to make a difference for those starfish one at a time. It would have helped if a marine biologist had come up with ways to pre-vent so many starfish from ending up on the shoreline and dying. (OK, that totally messes up the warm and fuzzy feeling in the story, and I may be oblivious to environmental system implications, but I hope you get my point nevertheless.)

SYSTEMIC CHANGE

In general, when it comes to the Christian community we don't normally think about how to change the world through the systems, structures and policies that govern the way our world runs. We don't think about changing the rules of how the game is played. Instead, we live inside those rules and we stay "grass roots" to work with people. We reach out to them with the gospel and we help care for the poor and underprivi-leged. I often hear, "It's all about people, it's all about people," which re-ally means, "Don't bother with the system, just try to help the people!" But in response, I want to exclaim, "Yes, but the systems affect people!"

Erika went to teach underprivileged children in New Orleans. After two very hard years of working in the city, she decided to go to graduate school in public policy. When I asked her why, she replied, "When I was teaching, I saw how hard life was on the kids, and as a teacher I wanted to do so much to help them. . . . But there was only so much I could do." She was finding that the teacher training programs often seemed pointless, the incentives for learning nonexistent, and day-to-day school life disempowering. She elaborated, "Now I want to change the system that makes it so hard for teachers to help their students. Plus, when I was there, I realized that I didn't want to just help my few students. I wanted to help every student in my district." Erika recognized just how much the lives of the underprivileged were affected by the policies enacted by those in power. The teachers, while working directly with the children, could only influence within the limits and framework set by the policymakers. And Erika found out that the educational policies and standards were especially burdensome for her as a teacher.

Michael Emerson and Christian Smith, in their provocative book *Divided by Faith: Evangelical Religion and the Problem of Race in America,* make some indicting statements about evangelical Christians. The history of the race problem in America shows an unfortunate pattern of white evangelical Christians doing nothing to change the status quo to help oppressed African Americans:

> White evangelicals, without any necessary intent, help to buttress the racialized society. Like their forbears during the Jim Crow segregation, who prescribed kindness toward people of other races and getting to know people across races, but did not challenge the Jim Crow system, present-day white evangelicals attempt to solve the race problem without shaking the foundations on which racialization is built. As long as they do not see or acknowledge the structures of racialization, they inadvertently contribute to them.[1]

The authors' point is that when it comes to the racial problems in our nation, white evangelicals have tended to deal with the problems by encouraging each other to make friendships across the racial barrier and to treat people kindly. While this is commendable, the same people do little to change the laws and policies that perpetuate so many of the racial problems. They do not challenge the status quo but seem content to let the system continue to run over people. It's easy for us to look back and say that the Jim Crow segregation laws were bad, but it's painful to acknowledge that evangelical Christians did little to overturn those laws. Even more painful to acknowledge are the ways we continue to turn a blind eye to current laws that systematically disfranchise poor minority communities.

Think about our churches. When was the last time you heard your pastor encourage you to get involved in the policies of the city in order to effect kingdom change for the poor? When was the last time your Christian community prayed for the men and women working in the confusing arena of politics? Think about the heroes of the Christian community. Are they not missionaries and full-time Christian workers like Hudson Taylor and Billy Graham? What about the Christians who are diligently working in politics and public policy? In some cases the changes they make will fill whole communities, even nations, with the fragrance of the kingdom—and the work of these fine men and women is rarely acknowledged as kingdom work.

I think of men like Frank Wolf (Republican) and Tony Hall (Democrat), who are believers working in Congress. Wolf has been cochair of the Congressional Human Rights Caucus, and Hall has been cochair of the Congressional Friends of Human Rights Monitors. Before the fall of Nicolae Ceausescu's dictatorship in Czechoslovakia, together they addressed human rights abuses there by bringing economic sanctions from the U.S. government. From their respective parties, they regularly use their influence to challenge abuses of power in international trade and to stand up for the poor. As you read this, they are wading through laws, lobbying fellow members of Congress and seeking out ways to affect the policies of our government so that God's peace and justice can come for masses of people. Some of us may never see the work that these men are doing, yet the pain of thousands and thousands of victims of poverty and abuse has been alleviated as a result of their work.

Wouldn't it be wonderful if churches started to pray for these men and women in political life as much as we pray for our missionaries? Wouldn't it be great if churches got involved in the public life of the community and advocated for the poor and oppressed?

It's not that I believe that the systems, structures and policies of society determine the direction of our lives. It's not that I believe that once we change the system, all will be well. I know that you cannot change people's hearts just by changing the social systems they live in. I know that we need to get up close, love people and encourage them to believe in Jesus. And I know that we need people working at the grass roots level to give direct aid to those in need. I know that systems can't *make* people good. However, the vision and mission of many churches do not address the systemic realities of how our world works. While proclaiming that people matter to God, we neglect the systems that often enslave and oppress them. Systems do matter. They may be invisible to most of us, but they have tremendous power to influence people's lives.

Seymour Williams is a physician who works in public health. While he spends a small portion of his week caring for individual patients at a community clinic, the bulk of his time is invested in research of public health issues. When he tries to explain why he is in public health as opposed to family practice, he explains:

> The analogy that I use is that I live downstream from a river that is contaminated by sewage, and the children are coming to you day in and day out and you are treating their diarrhea and you are saving their lives. That gets very tiring and you need a lot of people to help you save the kids with diarrhea. [So] you can go upstream and find out how [something] is dumping sewage into the stream and clean that out.[2]

For Seymour, public health is about cleaning up the sewage. Rather than simply responding to the effects of the contamination, Seymour is working to stop the contamination itself. In the same way, there are policies and structures "upstream" in our society that are producing pain and frustration for many people. In our kingdom vision to love people in God's name, is it not worth our time to go upstream and change those policies and structures so that the pain of many can be alleviated?

In our mission to seek the kingdom of God in our world, is it not part of our mission to seek the transformation of the systems and structures that powerfully affect the quality of life for people, especially for the poor and underprivileged? Is that not a part of what our King would desire for us to do in order to bring peace and justice to our world? In our desire to transform the world in Christ's name, we must lose our naive sentiment that it's all a matter of changing people one at a time. Look up at how the very systems we operate in have power for good or ill to influence the lives of people in our world. Look out at the poor and find out just how much the system influences their lives day to day. Look around and consider what the church can do to seek the kingdom of God around you.

CULTURAL CHANGE

It's not just the systems that work their invisible power on us. Other agents are invading our minds and hearts with dreams, visions and beliefs that often threaten to blind us to true reality and lead us on paths of destruction. These agents infiltrate our minds and take root in our hearts, and often they do it unbeknownst to us. They slip right past our defenses and get inside us. Sometimes these invisible forces push us toward God, while other times they clearly do not.

What are these agents? They make up our culture—the values, dreams and assumptions we take on by living in our land. As we participate in our culture, we imbibe ways of thinking, both good and bad, that color all we do. And through vehicles like media and education, these ways of thinking are transmitted to the masses. I once heard that if you really want to change the world, you should cause people to *think* the way you want them to. Have them see what you see and desire what you desire. Then you don't have to force them to do anything against their will; they will already *want* to do what you want them to do. Our culture—in both good ways and bad ways—is shaping the way we think about life.

The media. When it comes to the media, the power of transmission is that it's mostly visceral and deceptively indirect. It's about the motivations, dreams and values deep inside you. Rarely do messages come right out and say, "OK, we want you to waste your money and buy this product" or "We don't want you to believe there is only one God" or "Sex is the complete experience to solve all your problems." No, they slip in under the radar screen and make you feel a certain way about things or desire certain outcomes in your life. And pretty soon you are valuing what they value, desiring what they want you to desire and believing what they believe about life.

Our culture is permeated with a relativistic mindset that affirms that there is no one right way to "God" or "ultimate reality." In the end, we all walk our chosen paths and end up finding our own fulfillment. No one religious group can proclaim that the beliefs of other religious groups are wrong. As I often hear students say, "If Christianity is right for you, great! But just don't tell me that I'm going to hell if I don't believe in Jesus. What's right for you is right for you. It's not necessarily right for anyone else."

I face this all the time on campus. And as I dig underneath this persistent belief, I find that most students do not have any reasonable basis for their relativism. They have not thought through any sort of rationale as to why this sort of relativism is true. When I ask, "How do you know that we'll all be OK in the end? How do you know that there might not be three, or two, or maybe only one way that truly gets you to ultimate reality, to God? How do you know that there are multiple ways? How do you know that a relativistic way of thinking about religions reflects reality?" most students have no clear answers. They believe in relativism because they just "feel" that it has to be right. After all, they say, it's the more respectful thing to do. They don't seem to realize that it's not respectful at all to dismiss the distinctive beliefs of all the world religions and just say, "They're all the same," ignoring that some religions believe in a god while others don't believe that any type of god exists at all. They don't wonder, *What really happens when I die? Will I be reincarnated, face judgment or just disappear?* Something *does* happen; the question is, what is that something? It's not "all of the above"!

Although many high-level academic discussions about relativism take place in college philosophy and religion departments, most students have no clue about such discussions. Instead, they have simply absorbed the cultural value of religious relativism without really examining its merits.

How did this take such deep root in the minds of these students? One way is clearly through the media. Time and time again, the media paints ugly portraits of hatred and bigotry when religious groups, especially Christians, try to convert others. The models of love and tolerance perpetrated in the media are the people who let others keep to their chosen religious path. I remember seeing this in, of all places, a *Little House on the Prairie* episode. The villain in the story was a person who shunned and vilified Jews because he did not respect them. In the end, the wonderful and kind father, played by Michael Landon, showed the way—that of acceptance and tolerance. While nothing was said about the validity of truth claims, the impression left with the viewer was that any claim to know what is true and to declare another religion wrong is plain bigotry. And how can you not want to be as kind and gentle as Michael Landon?

We have cultural icons like Oprah Winfrey who preach their brand of spirituality to the masses. She encourages us to "get in touch with our spirit," never questioning whether our spirit is really connected to the Spirit of the true and living God. As a result, it seems ridiculous and outright mean for someone to believe that there is only one way to God. And so it *feels* wrong to proclaim a salvation only by the name of Jesus.

The media works its powerful effect in our lives so that we start believing certain things about life and adopting particular dreams and visions of success. We start dreaming about that wonderful life full of financial security, sex and travel, and those dreams squeeze out dreams for the kingdom of God. We start valuing tolerance and open-mindedness so much that we disregard the need to proclaim a unique Savior. We start seeing distorted portrayals of certain minority groups so that we fear them and retreat into our segregated havens. Before we realize it, we are believing lies and half-truths and are acting in ways that sabotage our ability to be salt and light for the kingdom of God.

Rather than retreating into holy bubbles meant to keep us pure (which, to be frank, I don't think is possible), ought we not bring the life-giving influence of the kingdom into the culture through the media? Wouldn't it be great if the media helped people to care about the plight of the poor? What if the voice of the media did a better job of building understanding between ethnic communities?

I recently watched *Remember the Titans*. In the movie, Denzel Washington plays a black coach who leads a football team of both black and white players to build bridges across the racial divide. The movie offers the viewer a vision of racial reconciliation that touches the heart and mind. It makes one feel the desire to bridge the divide that continues to stand between racial communities in our world today. We see the powerful effect the media can have to promote peace and reconciliation.

Is it not a part of the mission of the kingdom to influence and transform the culture-shaping vehicle of the media? I am concerned about the stigma attached to the media. Rather than coming alongside those in the media to influence them, Christians tend to fight them—boycotting offensive programs, complaining to officials about pornography and violence, and fearing the media's contamination. How many Christians ever consider becoming a change agent in the media? Journalists, advertising agents, actors and communication professionals are not the most glorified workers in the Christian community. And Christians who do enter those fields find an easier time gaining affirmation by using those skills in the Christian media rather than seeking to transform the respected media centers of the world.

But imagine what it would be like in a world where churches encouraged their young people to be journalism majors and have internships at international news agencies. Imagine what it would be like if Hollywood was filled with Christian actors, directors, screenwriters and producers all seeking to bring the fragrance of the kingdom into their craft. Can you see the potential of more and more movies and TV shows that influence our world toward kingdom values like reconciliation, care for the poor, justice for the oppressed, and the pursuit of truth?

Without dismissing the complexity of influencing the media, I do think that we need to consider the culture-shaping realm of media as a focus for mission and prayer. It deserves our brightest and best. And we ought to work hard not only to denounce what is sinful but also to affirm what is helpful in bringing greater understanding, peace and justice.

The university. Charles Malik wrote in his book *A Christian Critique of the University,* "The university is a clear-cut fulcrum with which to move the world."[3] What Malik recognizes is that modern universities have tremendous culture-shaping influence in our world. Mark Noll writes,

> The great institutions of higher learning in Western culture function as the mind of Western culture. They define what is important; they specify procedures to be respected; they set agendas for analyzing the problems of the world; they produce the books that get read and that over decades continue to influence thinking around the world—and they do these tasks not only for the people who are aware of their existence, but for us all.[4]

I think of watching the evening news. As the news correspondent presents the situation at hand, often the news story cuts away to an interview with a university professor that provides the "expert" perspective on the subject. This highlights the authoritative status of our universities. They help to define how our economy runs and how medical procedures are done. They give the definitive perspective on what's happened in history and what cultural trends indicate. We appeal to universities and their professors to get a better understanding of all aspects of life.

We may not be conscious of it, but many of the ways society runs have been influenced by the theories, intellectual developments and conclusions drawn by the men and women at our universities in years past. The very nature of the research university is to engage in research that will further the human experience. It's hard to comprehend just how much we have been influenced by the developments in the university. What they actually do may be so specialized that it makes no sense to the rest of us. But they do have a significant influence on the development of the human experience.

In college, I was a psychology major and studied the theories of men like Sigmund Freud. My appreciation for Freud was initially pretty low. After all, he wanted me to believe that I was secretly in love with my mother, motivated primarily by sex and duped into believing in God due to society's collective desire for a father figure. My appreciation, however, increased dramatically one day in class. My professor started rattling off various theories and principles (which I have long since forgotten!) that were basic to contemporary psychology. He then added, "They've all come to us, in one way or another, from Freud." The father of modern psychology was not as kooky as I thought him to be.

As I think back on my studies in psychology, I realize that most of the main figures of psychology were not people of Christian faith. Their understanding of the human experience did not take seriously the existence of a transcendent Creator who made us all in his image. Instead, they thought the concept of God might stem from wish fulfillment or unresolved issues from childhood, for example. And they reduced our nature to a combination of unresolved urges, childhood conflicts and identity issues rather than taking seriously our connectedness to a Creator. And to this day, much of psychological analysis continues to take its cues from men and women who have no place for God in the equation. So every counseling office, every psychiatric couch, every clinical analysis of people's psychological development has been marked to some degree by principles, theorems and frameworks that are devoid of God.

Granted, a growing number of gifted Christian psychologists are seeking to integrate their faith into their clinical practice. However, the authoritative voices in psychology are still those that leave God out of the equation. What would have happened if some of the leading voices in psychology were not just people like Freud but also Christian men and women? What if they posited theories about human development and psychosis that took spiritual reality seriously? What if they came to be respected as leading authorities in the world of psychology? What if *their* books came to be the established books read by every university student studying the enterprise of psychology? I'm not sure what it would look like, but psychological practice would clearly be different from what it is today.

In contrast to the current state of psychology, note the field of philosophy. Prior to the 1980s, many found it difficult to integrate Christian faith with the academic arena of philosophy. So many of the leading voices in philosophy were people without Christian faith. Yet in the '80s an amazing thing began to take place:

> Philosophical publications aimed at both scholarly and popular audiences forthrightly expounded classic Christian teaching as the basis for right thinking and right behavior. Essays defending some aspect of classical Christian dogma became the centerpiece of concentrated discussion in at least some philosophical quarterlies. A Society of Christian Philosophers was organized in 1978. Soon thereafter it began a quarterly, *Faith and Philosophy*, which rapidly established itself as a leading journal in the philosophy of religion. And meetings of the society, both regionally and nationally, have been scenes of considerable intellectual stimulation. In sum, the Christian philosophers had made their presence felt in the world of scholarship more substantially than intellectuals in any other discipline.[5]

In today's world, Christian philosophers like Alvin Plantinga, Nicholas Wolterstorff, Eleonore Stump, Basil Mitchell and William Alston have all become respected scholars of philosophy. Now philosophy students cannot help but grapple with the work of such men and women.

Whether we realize it or not, the academic voices of the university world often create an authoritative body of influence that trickles down to the daily practice of business, social science, historical analysis and so forth. And as Noll says, "They do these tasks not only for the people who are aware of their existence, but for us all."

Yet when it comes to the church's desire to influence our world, I rarely hear a call to pray for and transform the universities. Again, as in the case of systemic influences, the church seems blind to the society-shaping influence of our universities. But the need is great. Malik goes on to say,

> The university is a clear-cut fulcrum with which to move the world. The problem here is for the church to realize that no greater service can it render both itself and the cause of the gospel, with which it is entrusted, than to try to recapture the universities for Christ on whom they were all originally founded. . . . More potently than by any other means, change the university and you change the world.[6]

People like Charles Malik and Mark Noll understand that when you influence the universities you influence the world. The assumptions and beliefs of the university become the authoritative voices that tell the world what is right and true. The men and women who come out of the universities become the leaders and shapers of our world. The research and developments in our universities become the basis for established ways of doing things across society.

Yet I fear that for many, universities represent places of contamination for our youth, a place where their minds will be filled with atheistic ideology and their hearts pulled to drugs and sex. Without realizing the powerful influence that our universities have on society, we abandon them to the devil without considering whether God wants us to transform them into avenues of his grace and truth.

I don't want to dismiss the fact that countless students from Christian upbringings have walked onto campus only to graduate with no Christian faith at all. It grieves me to personally see some of these students walk away from God.

However, the answer is not to abandon our universities but to influence and change them. Historically, the case can be made that we *did* abandon the universities, and I wonder whether part of our current cultural disintegration is not a result of our exodus from them. Early in the 1900s, the church* saw how the universities were advocating ideologies that critically undermined Christian faith. Therefore, the Christians started leaving the universities. Faculty left to start Christian colleges and Bible schools, and Christian students followed them rather than going to the secular universities, where they feared contamination. Without the leaven of Christian influence, our universities, which had once been designed to raise up men and women of faith, soon became completely naturalistic in outlook. No longer did God even factor into a critical academic understanding of the universe. No longer were intellectual analysis and academic endeavor considered in service to God. Letting God into the picture was deemed primitive and nonintellectual.

And as the university went, so did culture at large. It was only a matter of time until the influence of our leading universities trickled into society through successive generations of students and their research. Leaders in society who came out of our universities carried the outlook of the university with them into business, the arts, social science, technology, medicine and education. And the authoritative resources that set the standard of the way things run also reflected the naturalism of the university.

---

*When I talk about the church, I am referring to the fundamentalist church and later the evangelical church that sought to stay faithful to the authority of the Scriptures and to the need for personal faith in Christ.

It's easy for me to be critical of what the church did in relation to the university in recent history. I wasn't there and don't understand what it was like from the inside. However, I look around right now and wonder how different life would be if Christians did not abandon the universities of our nation. And I look at our universities today and wonder how different society could be for future generations if this generation sought to influence the secular university rather than abandon it. Only time will tell.

But for me, regardless of the pragmatic implications, it goes back to the gospel of the kingdom. God wants to establish his reign over his world. Jesus did not come simply to rescue people from this world to whisk them off to heaven. He came so that the entire creation might be redeemed. As I think about the university, I think it is a place to redeem. Furthermore, it is a place *through which to redeem the rest of our world.* With its influential role in the development of society, does it not seem fitting that we affect the university so that it might further the redemption of the kingdom to the rest of the world?

We need men and women, both at the student level and at the faculty level, to incarnate the love and truth of the kingdom of God in our universities. We need Christian students to engage the academic and social life of the university with the redeeming influence of God's kingdom. We need Christian faculty to integrate their faith with their research and to serve God wholeheartedly in their professions. We need university administrators seeking to make the university a place where kingdom values take root.

Then imagine what it could be like. The textbooks that young people around the world study would be filled with the values and perspective of the kingdom. As the news story cuts away to the authority on the subject at hand, sharing her research on the topic would be a follower of Jesus who has become respected in her field as *the* leading expert. As students go to study at colleges and universities in our nation, their Christian faith would be respected and they would find encouragement to integrate their faith into their studies. As companies look to gain research on certain business practices, implicit in the research would be a value for ethics and consideration for the poor. In fact, practically every area of life would be influenced by the Christian faith and its integration into the academic research and learning of the university world.

CONCLUSION

The gospel is about God establishing his reign over all his creation, so the mission of the gospel ought to be concerned with the transformation of culture-shaping forces like the media and the university. Not only are these places that need the redeeming influence of the kingdom, they are also powerful avenues through which the fragrance of the kingdom can be spread throughout our world. Peter Kreeft writes,

> Treatment of a disease is always most effective if it is applied to the source of the disease itself, rather than somewhere else, later and further down the line of dominoes that the disease has already knocked down. In other words, to cure this social disease we must infiltrate its social sources. To put it clearly and bluntly, we must infiltrate the psychology and sociology departments, along with the popular journalism and media production centers, that is, the mind-molding areas of the battlefield. The most powerful forces in America are no longer church and state but Harvard and Hollywood.[7]

When you have a truncated gospel, you have truncated mission. When the gospel is all about the salvation of lost individuals, then the mission of the gospel is all about reaching out to those lost individuals. We do our best to reach out to people, one by one by one. Yet when the gospel is about the kingdom of God, the mission of the gospel starts to take on all sorts of new dimensions. No longer is it just about helping individuals find salvation in Jesus. It is also about bringing the loving reign of God wherever there is the darkness of sin and death.

As we think about what that means today, it helps us integrate our own life more holistically, and it refocuses our eyes on areas traditionally over-looked by a more individualistic gospel. The gospel also does the following:

- It clarifies what it means for each of us, as men and women of the kingdom, to be in mission. As we live out our day-to-day lives, it is not only in the evangelistic encounters that the mission of the gospel takes place. The mission of the gospel goes forth whenever and wher-ever we flesh out the kingdom of God and spread its influence.

- It brings together a concern for conversion with a concern for peace and justice in our world. The mission of the kingdom is not just about saving souls but also about feeding the poor, addressing in-justice and speaking about the social issues that plague our society. Rather than prioritizing evangelism above other aspects of the church's mission, the mission of the kingdom brings it all together into an integrated whole. Now the mission of the kingdom is to seek the redemption of our world wherever the Old Age of sin and death manifests itself.

- It brings into focus a need to open our eyes to the systemic realities of our society. Rather than just working at the grass roots level where problems manifest themselves, we need to take on the sys-tems and policies that produce the problems that surface at the grass roots level. The mission of the kingdom opens up a whole new di-mension of what local churches ought to consider as they reach out to their communities with the life-giving message of the gospel. It draws our attention to a whole new breed of missionaries: those working in the confusing arenas of politics and public policy with the goal of being agents of the kingdom of God.

- It brings into focus a need to transform the culture-shaping institu-tions of our world. As we seek to bring the springtime of God's king-dom, we need to take seriously how the media and universities of our world transmit values and dreams that infiltrate the minds and hearts of us all. We need missionaries of the kingdom who will boldly enter the fields of journalism, advertising, entertainment, communications, university education and university administration with a calling to be salt and light. We need generations of university students who engage the academic and social life on campus with the love and truth of the gospel.

As we pray "Your kingdom come. Your will be done, on earth as it is in heaven," let us work to see that kingdom fleshed out more fully.

PART FOUR

THE KINGDOM
AND EVANGELISM

10

LIVING IN THE MATRIX

MORPHEUS: I imagine that right now you're feeling a bit like Alice, tumbling down the rabbit hole.

NEO: You could say that.

MORPHEUS: I can see it in your eyes. You have the look of a man who accepts what he sees because he is expecting to wake up. Ironically, this is not far from the truth. Do you believe in fate?

NEO: No.

MORPHEUS: Why not?

NEO: Because I don't like the idea that I'm not in control of my life.

MORPHEUS. I know exactly what you mean. Let me tell you why you're here. You're here because you know something. What you know, you can't explain; but you feel it. You've felt it your entire life. That there's something wrong. You don't know what it is, but it's there. Like a splinter. Driving you mad. It is this feeling that has brought you to me. Do you know what I'm talking about?

NEO: The Matrix?

MORPHEUS: Do you want to know what it is? [Neo nods.] That Matrix is everywhere. It is all around us. Even now in this very room. You can see it when you look out your window or when you turn on your television. You can feel it *when you go to work. When you go to church. When you pay your taxes. It is the world that has been pulled over your eyes to blind you from the truth.*

NEO: What truth?

MORPHEUS: That you are a slave, Neo. Like everyone else, you were born into bondage. Born into a prison that you cannot smell or taste or touch. A prison of your mind. Unfortunately, no one can be told what the Matrix is. You have to see it for yourself. This is your last chance. After this, there is no turning back. You take the blue pill, the story ends. You wake up in your bed and believe whatever you want to believe. You take the red pill, you stay in Wonderland and I show you how deep the rabbit hole goes. Remember, all I'm offering is the truth. Nothing more. Follow me.

In the movie *The Matrix*, everyone is born into a world where they are enslaved and they don't even know it. Morpheus knows the truth and frees others like Neo. Neo's eyes are then opened and he sees the truth. He becomes free of the deception and heads down the road of battling the forces of the Matrix.

Isn't all of this a bit like the kingdom of God? Because of the Fall, everyone is born into slavery—slavery to sin, death and the god of this age (Ephesians 2:1-3). And most people don't even know their predicament. But Jesus has come to free men and women from their enslavement and to send them to invite others into the freedom of the kingdom of God.

Living in the kingdom of God gives us new eyes to see the world around us. In 2 Corinthians 5:16-17 Paul writes,

> From now on, therefore, we regard no one from a human point of view; even though we once knew Christ from a human point of view, we know him no longer in that way. So if anyone is in Christ, there is a new creation: everything old has passed away; see, everything has become new!

In some translations (like the NIV), verse 17 reads, "If anyone is in Christ, *he is* a new creation" (emphasis added). Yet in the original Greek the phrase is literally, "If anyone is in Christ, new creation," and a good case can be made that it should be translated as the NRSV has it: "If anyone is in Christ, *there is* a new creation" (emphasis added).* Paul is saying that anyone who has put faith in Jesus has been ushered into a whole new creation, the new reality of the present but growing kingdom of God. Therefore, that individual's perspective ought to be radically different from when he or she was not in the kingdom. It's not just that a person is new, but rather that a whole new reality, the kingdom of God, has begun in Jesus Christ. And each person who puts faith in Jesus has been born anew into the reality of the kingdom of God. That's what Paul is talking about, and it's why he can no longer look at Christ and others the same way.

Before becoming a Christian, Paul saw Christ "from a human point of view." He must have looked at Jesus as some failed Messiah wannabe whose followers were now leading Jews astray from the covenant of Israel. But then he met Jesus—or perhaps I should say Jesus met him! Paul was knocked to the ground on the way to Damascus and confronted by the reality of who Jesus really is (Acts 9). And so Paul surrendered to the King and entered the kingdom of God. His perspective of Jesus was irrevocably transformed, along with his perspective of everyone else.

I think that evangelism starts with a changed perspective through the eyes of the kingdom of God. Like Neo in *The Matrix,* like Paul in his conversion, our eyes have been opened. Now we see the world differently. Once Neo's eyes were opened, he understood that people are enslaved and that everyone is hooked up inside the Matrix, totally oblivious to their predicament. Once Paul's eyes were opened, he saw that people apart from Christ are slaves to sin and destined for a godless eternity. He

---

*New Testament scholars Ralph P. Martin, Word Biblical Commentary (vol. 40); Victor Paul Furnish, The Anchor Bible (*II Corinthians*); and Linda Belleville, The IVP New Testament Commentary Series (*2 Corinthians*) are among the advocates of this view.

even tells us in 2 Corinthians 4:4 that people who don't know Jesus are blinded by the god of this age.

We forget kingdom reality and let our vision get clouded by the hustle and bustle of our everyday lives. We lose sight of the gravity of reality and forget the lostness of the Old Age that Jesus has conquered. When I see non-Christians enjoying material abundance and professional success, it becomes easy for me to lose sight of kingdom reality. I forget the truth that apart from Jesus, they are objects of wrath due to their sin and headed for an eternity apart from God and his goodness. I forget that the abundant life is ultimately found only in Jesus Christ. It is only when the kingdom of God breaks into my horizon that I remember. As I hear God's Word speak to me, as I experience the goodness of Christ-centered fellowship, when I am a part of God's work to see justice and reconciliation spread in our world—*then* I am reminded of kingdom truth, and only *then* do I see clearly and understand the true nature of life around me.

I think one of the keys to maintain kingdom vision, to see clearly, is to practice spiritual disciplines. I talked earlier about how the Holy Spirit has been given to us to guide and empower us to live out the kingdom life while we await the kingdom's consummation at Jesus' return. I pointed to spiritual disciplines as the tools we have to keep in touch with the Holy Spirit. As we consider how we are to see clearly, the Spirit of God clears away the fuzziness through the spiritual disciplines and refocuses our vision to see kingdom reality clearly, to see the truth about people's situations apart from Christ. As I daily spend time with God to listen to Scripture, engage in prayer and meditate on God's work in my life, I gain kingdom perspective. Without those times, I tend to exist in a sort of unending dash through life, with all of its storms and pressures shaping my vision rather than the truth about the salvation and life found only in Jesus Christ and the kingdom of God.

Are your eyes open? Do you see with kingdom vision? You have been rescued from the dominion of darkness and brought into the kingdom of God in Jesus Christ (Colossians 1:13). You now stand in the freedom of God's reign, no longer a slave to sin destined for God's wrath. Yet people around you are still enslaved to sin and headed for a godless eternity. Do you see?

THE BLINDNESS

As we look around at our world with our kingdom vision, we see people who are lost in their sin, headed to a godless eternity, without the abundant life of the kingdom of God, without the hope of the kingdom to come—and for the most part, *they have no idea what they are missing!* Paul says that the god of this age has blinded the minds of people in this world so that they just cannot see the truth. We have been sent to help them see.

We know that the problem is sin—that by choosing to live for ourselves rather than for God we are all sinners who need our sin to be dealt with. We are sinners whom God rightfully should punish. Yet though we are sinners, Christ died for us so that through him we might find freedom from sin and experience the kingdom life we were always meant for. But how do you convince people that they are sinners in need of Christ's redemption?

One major struggle in evangelism continues to be the task of convincing non-Christians that they even need Jesus. For Christians, it's clear that everyone needs Jesus because we are all sinners. We have rebelled against God, and the consequences of our rebellion are alienation from God and from one another; our entire world order is off-balance with pain, suffering and injustice. All of creation is under the bondage of death and sin. As men and women who have rebelled against God, apart from Jesus Christ we are all headed to a godless eternity. So from inside the Christian story, it is abundantly clear just how much we need Jesus. But how do you convince postmodern non-Christian men and women, many of whom have had little exposure to the Bible, that they need Jesus?

Often, when people share the message of Jesus they seek first to establish the fact that we are all sinners in need of grace and forgiveness. And it is commonly thought that sin means breaking God's rules and failing to measure up to his standards. Therefore, a popular strategy to communicate this idea is to help people realize just how high God's standards are and how low our performance is. At an evangelistic outreach, one speaker laid out a graph of goodness. On the low end was Adolf Hitler. Much higher up on the graph was Mother Teresa. Then he invited us to visualize where we would fit on the graph of goodness. Everyone sees themselves as being higher than Hitler but not nearly as high as Mother Teresa. Then the speaker opened up the graph to reveal that what God required of us to get into heaven was miles and miles higher than even Mother Teresa. All of this was meant to show us that none of us measures up to God's perfect standard of goodness, so we are unable to get to heaven on our own.

While this clearly articulates the truth about our failure to measure up, I've always felt that such presentations of sin just don't hit home with me, and I suspect that they don't hit home with other people either. In my experience, when I try to help students see their sinfulness as that of not measuring up to God's standards, it doesn't connect with their heart of hearts. It might make sense to them in their head, but it just doesn't tap into something inside them that says, "Gosh, I'm in trouble! I need to find out more!" Instead, it simply evokes a response of "Hmmm . . . that's an interesting way of looking at things."

When I try to put myself in a non-Christian's shoes as I listen to all of this, it feels a bit arbitrary. It feels as if this measuring stick of goodness has been set by some outside standard-maker to make their point and lure me into compliance. It doesn't resonate internally with our current ideas of goodness. After all, in a postmodern generation of relationships and tolerance, the only real "sins" are murder, bigotry and intolerance. As long as you have not killed someone, lashed out violently in bigotry or slandered someone's lifestyle or religion, you are doing fine.* So when

---

*This is why Christianity already has huge obstacles to overcome with emerging generations of students. Christianity has been linked to oppressive colonialism, oppression of women and homosexuals, judgment of all other religions, and validation of white supremacist groups. Christianity is guilty of the major "sins" of our postmodern culture!

we try to convince non-Christians that they are sinners who have failed to reach God's standards of goodness, it often *feels* unconvincing. It makes *logical* sense that if we have not attained perfect standards of goodness then we cannot enter the heaven of a good and perfect God. But intuitively, it misses the heart experience of non-Christian students and therefore often falls flat and is unconvincing. People just don't *feel* that guilty before God.

I suspect that in previous generations, this approach to communicating our sinfulness worked and persuasively convinced people that they needed a Savior. The Judeo-Christian moral ethic was the dominant framework for society. Everyone knew what "sin" was. Everyone here in the West, whether Christian or not, had some sense of Christian moral principles. The landscape was clear—you knew where the boundaries were that separated good from bad, right from wrong. And people knew that they weren't perfect; they knew that at different points of their life they had stepped over the line and transgressed the laws of goodness. So when we led them to the cross, their hearts pounded with excitement at the discovery of a way to deal with their missteps and transgressions.

Nowadays, however, the rules of morality are up for grabs. Beyond the moral law against murder, bigotry and intolerance, what moral rules does all of society agree to? The landscape is no longer clear. Boundaries between good and bad, right and wrong are now thought to be a matter of personal opinion. As a result, no one really *feels* deep down that he is a "sinner" in need of forgiveness, at least not a sinner in the sense of someone who has broken God's laws and not measured up to his standards of goodness. No one *feels* as if she is a sinner who is guilty enough to deserve hell and judgment.

Notice that I say that they don't *feel* that this is so. We may explain that God's standards are perfect and that none of us measures up. But in our cultural morass of individualism and relativistic thinking, it just doesn't *feel* true. What feels true is that we are basically good people who deserve to be happy. So when we try to help people see that they are sinners, it sounds arbitrary; it doesn't resonate with the struggles and longings deep within their hearts.

Isn't there a more effective way to convince people that they need Jesus? Is sin simply about breaking God's laws? As I have thought about the good news of the kingdom, I have begun to use a different approach in telling students about Jesus.

The creation-wide reach of the kingdom highlights that it is not just individuals who are lost but a whole creation. Every aspect of life is tainted by the effects of humanity's sin and rebellion. We look out at the world and see violence and injustice. We look at our relationships and see pain and brokenness. We look within and feel our incompleteness and emptiness. We walk through life and experience uncontrollable tragedies and catastrophes. Wherever we turn, we see that *something is wrong with this place!* I believe that deep down we all know that things are not right. As I talk to non-Christians, I often ask, "Could it be that this sense that something is not right indicates that you were made for something more?" The questions are, What exactly is wrong? Why is life this way? Is there anything we can do to deal with it?

In terms of evangelism, this intuitive feeling that there is something wrong with life is a question that is just begging to be answered. And it is this intuitive feeling that serves as an on-ramp for the good news of the gospel. All of this leads naturally to talking about God's good creation and how humanity threw it all away when they rebelled against God. When I talk about sin, I don't focus on sin as breaking God's laws. Rather, I talk about sin as the internal heart attitude that says, "I will live *my* life *my* way!" Sin is about refusing to live under the good and loving reign of God our Creator and King. Not only does this accurately describe what happened in the Garden of Eden with Adam and Eve, it also resonates with how every non-Christian tends to live today. Furthermore, it more naturally follows that the decision to turn away from sin is a decision to embrace the kingship of Jesus, to no longer live life according to one's own designs but to live life unreservedly for the Lord Jesus and his kingdom.

I have found that this speaks to many people. Although they aren't anxious about how far they've fallen short of standards of righteousness, they are conscious of how broken life is. The brokenness of life is a near-daily experience, whether it's fighting with a dating partner, feeling depressed or seeing a world gone crazy on the nightly news. When sin is reframed in terms of a lifestyle attitude that disregards God, people see and understand their own guilt. As students who know the brokenness of life are confronted with their rebellion against their Creator, the good news of the kingdom not only *feels* like good news, it also leads them toward a pathway of discipleship, obedience and mission.

I have found the following outline effective for sharing the story of the gospel.

1. Something's not right with us and our world.

- We feel it when our lives don't "work": tragedies hit, suffering persists or we feel deep within that something is wrong, even if on the outside all is going pretty well.

- We feel it in relationships that are full of brokenness, pain and heartache.

- We see it in the world around us. Violence, corruption, injustice and environmental disintegration are all over. Sometimes improvements are made (for example, diminished threat of nuclear war), yet great evil and pain mark humanity's existence and continue to plague us no matter what we do. Even with the advances we make in education, technology and scientific understanding, we cannot seem to fix all the things that are wrong with our world.

    The sense we have that not everything is right often leads us to ask why. What can we do about it?

As a Christian, I believe that this is not the way it was supposed to be, nor is this the way it will always be.

2. The world was meant to be good.

- In the beginning God set up our world, and it was all good. It resonated with peace, justice and love. Humans were in right relationship with God and each other, and in peaceful partnership with the environmental order.

3. Sin and its effects distorted the world we live in now.

- Humans decided that they wanted to live life their own way, regardless of what God wanted. They felt that they knew what would make them happy, so they chose to rebel against God.

- In the same way that putting water in the gas tank of your car causes the entire car to malfunction, humanity's choice to rebel against God affected all aspects of God's good creation, destroying its God-given harmony. Our life with God, with each other and with the entire created order was tragically distorted. Human rebellion is like putting water in the gas tank of the universe.

- We continue to feel the effects of human rebellion today as we see and feel that things are not right in our world. And we continue the human rebellion as we choose to live life for ourselves rather than in loving service to God.

4. In Jesus, God has taken the initiative to fix what we broke.

- *Jesus as the answer.* God could have left his creation in this sorry state, but because he loved us he chose to help us. God came to us in Jesus Christ. Jesus was the visible face of our invisible God. And he came to call us back home to himself.

- *Jesus' life.* Jesus came and announced that through him God was beginning to reclaim his lost creation. He demonstrated this as he healed sicknesses, banished evil spirits and forgave people of their sins. He partied with the partygoers and hung out with prostitutes and outcast members of society to show that God's love was for all people.

- *Jesus' death.* When Jesus died on the cross, he died in our place. Because we chose to live life for ourselves, we were guilty of rebellion against God. Jesus' death, in a mysterious way, took on the punishment for our rebellion. The Bible even says he became a curse for us.

- *Jesus' resurrection.* On the third day after his death, God made Jesus alive again. His resurrection validated his claims and provided us with a tangible picture of the new and enduring life that he calls all of us into.

5. God will one day make all things right.

- One day Jesus will come back to finish the work of reclaiming God's creation, and everything will resonate with God's love, peace and justice.

- Those who choose to follow God as he is revealed in Jesus Christ will enter into this new creation, but those who choose to reject God's initiative through Jesus will continue in eternal separation from God and his goodness.

6. Meanwhile, God continues to redeem his creation in the present.

- God is always at work to continue reclaiming his lost creation. So he is calling men and women into communities where barriers of race, status and gender no longer keep people apart: communities that tell of his love and stand for his justice. Through these communities, God is at work to bring healing and peace to all creation.

7. *You can respond to God's offer of new life.*

- Turn away from living life for yourself.

- Accept what God did for you by Jesus' life, death and resurrection.

- Commit to living your life for God, for his justice, peace and reconciliation.

- Join God's family, the community of peace and justice.

Once we regain a more biblical understanding of the gospel as the good news of the inbreaking kingdom of God, our evangelism looks quite different from the boxed-in version we've confined ourselves to in our recent past. Furthermore, as we regain a gospel of the kingdom, we find new ways to connect with the hearts and minds of a postmodern generation that is lost and adrift, headed toward a Christless eternity.

EVANGELISM: TELLING THE ULTIMATE TRUE STORY

In the movie *The Matrix*, everyone is living a lie. They live out their day-to-day lives as if what they see is what is true. Yet Neo stumbles onto the Matrix, and then all of these weird, unexplainable events shatter his world as he pursues the meaning of the Matrix. A climactic event comes when Trinity and Morpheus confront Neo with the truth: It's all a lie. Life is not what it seems. Everyone thinks they are free, but in truth they are all slaves. Morpheus offers Neo the way to experience the truth—the red pill. If Neo takes the blue pill, he'll wake up with a bad headache and he won't remember what's happened. But if Neo takes the red pill, he'll be swept up into the truth.

I think evangelism is like Morpheus and Trinity helping this "seeker," Neo, to find the truth about life and reality. God, in Jesus, has shown us that the truth about life and reality is that Jesus has come to establish God's kingdom and free us from our bondage to sin, death and Satan. But no one knows this. We *appear* to be free, but most people move through life oblivious to the truth about God and his kingdom. We're in the middle of an unfolding drama in which our choices and decisions about Jesus make an eternal, life-transforming difference for our present as well as our future. And we are inviting people to understand the true nature of this drama and to enter in, living life according to this new understanding about life, history and the future.

Right now I am reading a fictional novel about ancient lords and kingdoms. It's about a noble family who find themselves caught in a battle for the throne. The good king has died, and the dark queen is bringing her plans to fruition to have her family take over the throne. Already one good noble has been assassinated because he tried to unearth the queen's designs. The father of this noble family has been imprisoned; the wife and son are now gathering forces for battle. And a third enemy army is preparing to enter the fray to take over. All along the way, there are strange deaths and mysterious disappearances that are yet to be resolved.

I don't know the ending. My guess is that this noble family will somehow emerge victorious, but I don't know how and I don't know for certain. I don't know whether any of the family members will die, nor do I know what the reason is for all of these strange deaths and disappearances. As I jump back into the story each night, I feel the drama of the story. I feel the tension of heading into battle not knowing whether the imprisoned father will survive. I feel all of the twists and turns, all of the ups and downs.

Now what if the author of the story magically transported himself into the story to tell the characters the ending? What if the author appeared in the prison next to the good father and said, "Don't worry, it will all work out. The queen will be overthrown. Just hang on. Don't give in to the queen's intimidation!"

Isn't that what the gospel is? Here we are, living in God's story as his kingdom moves toward its fulfillment and consummation. God has stepped into the story in Jesus to tell us what is going on. He's told us the good news of how it will end. And he's called us to hang on, to not give in to the temptation to lose hope. What's more, the author of the story is also the hero of the story. He's stepped in and gone to battle for us. Jesus went to war and won the decisive victory through his death and resurrection that secured victory for all who believe. This is the good news for those of us who are still in the story.

Most of our world has no idea that the story of the kingdom is the true story about life and history. And they go through life believing counterfeit stories that lead them astray. Yet deep inside they are searching to find the true story, a story that we were all created to live by. John F. Alexander frames his wonderful book *The Secular Squeeze: Reclaiming Christian Depth in a Shallow World* around the idea that our secular culture has left us with hollow stories that leave us empty and often bored:

> Deep down we know that something is wrong, but we're at a loss to know what to do about it. We throw ourselves further into our work or studies, we go to marriage renewal weekends, we jog, we have affairs, we try the church, we begin to meditate. Some things help, but nothing makes the difference. Gnawing emptiness remains, and nothing seems to fill it.
>
> Hollowness within and hollowness without, a people and a culture with all the depth, all the mystery, all the passion gone. . . .
>
> God gave us the gift of hollowness to goad us and guide us toward him. It's like a compass: when we're going the wrong direction, when we're worshipping something less than God, we feel dissatisfied. We're haunted by the sense that we are not yet serving anything worthy of worship, not yet serving anything worthy of who we're meant to be.[1]

His book opens up the stories that have been imprinted on our life by our times and culture. And all the while, he challenges us to regain a sense of the Christian story.

Look around at our world! Some are banking on the hope that their hard work will pay off in happiness and security. Others are resting on the assumption that all things will work out in the end no matter what one believes about spiritual truth. Others wonder whether this life has only tragic endings. All of their hopes and dreams have been dashed on the rocks of hardship, and they've lost hope for happy endings. Wherever people are, I think that everyone is looking for stories to live by.

None of them realize that their place in God's story depends on their response to Jesus Christ. Jesus has come to establish his kingdom that will never end. He has died on the cross to free us from our bondage to sin, death and Satan. And he has called each of us to follow him as he continues to work out his plan for the kingdom. If we do not follow Jesus, we will find ourselves outside of the kingdom and banished from his love and goodness forever. But that depends on what we do now. Will we believe that God's story is the true story and choose to follow it? Or will we choose to follow our own story and make our own way, only to find ourselves in a Christless eternity?

Once people see and embrace the true story, their lives cannot but be changed. It's not as if they can say, "Wow, I get it!" and then go on living life the way they have been living it. Neo could not just go back into the life he knew as normal once he swallowed the red pill and saw the truth. No, once people see and embrace the story, they start living differently as they see the kingdom all around them.

I choose to tell the gospel as a big story, the story of salvation from creation to revelation. It is the overarching story of what God has done in the past, is doing now and will finish one day. Doing this reframes how one looks at life and beckons the listener to jump in. Because this story is true, everything changes.* The future is secured and the present is filled with new significance. This is a large, wonderful, true story that one can live by! It gives life hope and meaning, and it opens up vision for being a part of something of transcendent significance.

Yet the gospel is often understood and presented not as a story but as a set of propositional statements of truth about a past historical event:

- God is perfectly holy, just and loving.

---

*Here is where apologetics is needed to show that the story is *true*.

- We are sinners who cannot be in the presence of a holy and just God.

- God, in love for us, paid the price for our sins by sending Jesus to die on the cross.

- If we believe in Jesus, we can be forgiven of our sins and have eternal life with God.

While these propositions are true, they flatten the story. You line up the statements one way—without Jesus—and the result is death and hell. You line them up another way—putting Jesus in—and the result is salvation and heaven. Or if it is looked at as a story, it's often told as a story that happened two thousand years ago that is supposed to have implications for us today. It is not a story that is continuing right now and continues into our future. It's not a story we are being called *into*. As a result, it is stripped of some of its life-transforming power.

Our heart yearns for a story big enough to live by and true enough to carry us into eternity. So often in evangelical practice we proclaim a set of propositional statements or doctrinal truths and ask, "Do you believe these to be true?" Instead we should be proclaiming the drama of God's kingdom invading our world to move toward complete restoration and renewal, the only true story that can meet us in our hollowness and carry us through into forever. We've been given an incredible story of a kingdom that will never end, a story of hope and victory, a story of passion and love. And what's more, it's *true!* Ought we not invite others into this incredible story?

Conclusion

The gospel is the story of a good King who has come to reign. In love, he has come to restore his justice, peace and love in a world gone mad. He has battled the enemy and won the decisive victory that will secure the enemy's defeat. And we are on the way to the day when he will reign and everything will resonate with his blazing goodness.

Evangelism, therefore, is not simply calling people to believe in a historical event or in some doctrinal truths. Evangelism is telling the world this wonderful story and inviting men and women to enter into it. We are calling people to embrace this good King and submit to his good reign. We are calling them to live by this story before it is too late. Let's be faithful to live and tell the story!

11

CONVERSION?

Good King Richard has returned from battle. Robin Hood and his merry men accompany their beloved king as he heads home to his castle. They exult in the good news that Prince John will soon be stripped of his power and judged for his corruption and injustice. The goodness and justice of King Richard will soon be restored and the people will find peace.

What would you do if you lived back then and found out that King Richard had returned? I think that news would begin to spread from hamlet to village—"Good King Richard has returned!" Excitement would build as people saw the imminent end to their oppressive misery. People would begin to live differently in anticipation of King Richard's rule.

Isn't that a bit what evangelism is like when the good news of the kingdom of God is understood more clearly?

Our good King, the Lord Jesus, the ruler of all creation, has indeed returned and come to restore his good intentions for creation. He has come to judge evil, pay for our sinful rebellion and establish his reign of peace, love and justice. The end to the bitter reign of sin, death and Satan has been pronounced through Jesus' cross and resurrection. Jesus is on the way to his final coronation on the last day, when the trumpets will blow, the dead in Christ will rise up, and every knee will bow at the name of our King, the Lord Jesus. And now here we are, still on the road to Jesus' coronation with the good news that the King has come.

Evangelism is about proclaiming this good news about Jesus and his kingdom, a kingdom that has come, is present now and is still on its way. And I believe that without seeing the big picture of the kingdom, we wind up with misconceptions about evangelism.

I remember my college friend Sandy (not her real name). In my mind, as I worked to help people move toward conversion, I conceptualized conversion as believing in the truth of Jesus as a real person who had come to die on the cross for our sins. So as I shared my faith with Sandy, my goal was to hear her say, "Yes, I believe in Jesus, that he died for my sins." Sandy started inquiring about my faith early in my senior year in college, so we started meeting regularly to talk about Christ and read materials that would help her understand the Christian faith. We had great conversations about God, the Scriptures and the life of faith. It seemed that Sandy was just soaking it all in. At one point later in the year, I came out and asked her, "Sandy, you've been hearing all of this stuff for a while now. What do you think about Jesus now?" She responded, "Well, before, I just believed it was all a bunch of fairy tales and myths out to oppress people, but now . . . I guess I believe it's true." With a bit of excitement I asked, "Does that mean that you believe that Jesus died on the cross for your sins, Sandy?" "Yes," she replied. There it was! There was the statement that I had been working for in all of my evangelism.

So I tentatively declared, "Then, Sandy, I think you are a Christian!" So far so good, right? Well, not really. There was a problem. As we kept talking, it became clear that while Sandy believed that Jesus had died on the cross for her sins, she felt no qualms about continuing to have sex with her boyfriend. After all, she loved the guy, it felt great, and now her sins were forgiven so everything was covered.

Was Sandy a Christian or not? What's your call?

In retrospect I know that I could have done a better job of laying out the costs of discipleship and explaining more fully what it means to follow Jesus as Lord. But I unwittingly had led her down a road toward conversion without a clear picture of what conversion really is. Is conversion an intellectual assent to the truth of what Christ did on the cross? If it is more, then what exactly is that "more" that is required for a person to really become a Christian?

I wonder how different it would have been if I had told her the bigger story about God's kingdom that had come, is here and is yet to be fulfilled. What would have happened if I had talked more about Jesus as a king who had come to rule, rather than simply about a Jesus who came to pay for her sins? What if I had told her that the main idea of the gospel was that Jesus had come to break the power of sin and establish God's good reign over all creation—over every relationship, every individual life, all social systems and cultures, every nook and cranny of life? While the forgiveness of sins is wonderful news indeed, it's a part of a greater message about a King who has come to banish evil and reclaim his lost world.

Sandy still may have chosen to sleep with her boyfriend and live according to her own rules and desires. But I don't believe that either of us would have wondered whether she had really become a Christian. Inherent in a message about a king come to reign is the idea that those who come to this king must choose whether to serve him. There is no fuzzy never-never land where intellectual assent might be considered saving faith. There is no confusion about what believing in Jesus and entering the kingdom of God means: it's submitting to his authority as King. You choose either to become a Christian and enter the kingdom of God by pledging allegiance to Jesus as King or to reject the gospel message and live life according to your own designs. This clarifies what it means to become a Christian.

As I think about how many Christians conceive of conversion, the paramount issue is faith versus works. Salvation is about what God has done for us and not what we have done ourselves to earn it. Therefore, the decision to become a Christian must be stripped of any hint that we are "working" for our salvation. The gospel is seen exclusively through the lens of justification by faith; Jesus paid the price that we could never pay and lived a life of godliness that we could never live. Therefore, our response of faith is simply to *receive* the gift of Jesus' work for us. There must be no hint that we are working our way into faith or earning our way into salvation. The gospel is purely about God's grace that we receive. Jesus has done all the work; we simply receive it. I've even heard a gospel summary built around the concept of "do" versus "done." The bad news is that nothing we can *do* will ever be enough, but the good news is that all that is required has already been *done* for us by Jesus Christ on the cross. Therefore, the decision to follow Jesus is seen primarily as a decision to believe that Jesus did die on the cross for human sin and to receive the historical act as something done for each individual.

While I would never deny the truth of God's grace communicated in all of this, it has the feeling of reducing the message to a simple accounting transaction. The conversion process is seen as retabulating the ledger's balance so that our sins are no longer held against us. On the plus side, we get to put Jesus. He becomes our righteousness, so we receive righteous standing before a just and holy God. On the debt side, we get to cancel all debts because Jesus has already paid the debt for us.

The problem that I see is that the life of discipleship and mission is not inherent in this picture of the gospel. As seen in what happened with my friend Sandy, the response to the gospel does not inherently lead to one of commitment, trust and mission to a lost world. After all, the most important issue is to get your sins taken care of so that you can get to heaven. Author and philosopher Dallas Willard refers to this presentation of the gospel as a "gospel of sin management." The worst-case scenario can be seen in all of the men and women who early in life made some decision to "believe in Jesus and his cross." They raised their hand at a youth rally to "accept Christ," or they walked down the aisle when the preacher gave the altar call to "get saved." Yet now they live their life no differently than the person who never made a profession of faith in the Lord Jesus. While there may be tinges of guilt at how their life looks right now, they hold the as-

surance deep in their heart that their destiny in heaven is secured. After
all, they believe that Jesus died for them, and they indicated that with a
raised hand, a walk forward down the aisle, a "sinner's prayer." Therefore,
they believe that their sins are forgiven—past, present, future.

Any responsible Christian who shares the gospel would quickly clar-
ify that a part of the decision to receive Jesus' work on the cross is to respond with a commitment to follow Jesus as Lord out of gratitude for all
that he has done. We work hard to follow up a person's conversion with
intentional discipleship to show the new Christian what it means to live
out the Christian life under Jesus' lordship. We teach them spiritual disciplines and get them involved in a community of faith.

Yet in the most common conceptions of the gospel message, the inherent idea is to clear up one's sin/righteousness account by receiving
what's already been done on the cross. One receives this by "believing"
in it and accepting it as a gift.

Compare this to the idea inherent in what it means to respond to the
good news of the kingdom of God. When the good news is that Jesus has
come to free us from our bondage to sin and death and to establish his
reign of peace, love and justice over all his creation, it dramatically fills out
the picture of what conversion means. It puts the grace versus works message in perspective. The good news of the kingdom is about a King who
has come to reign and is advancing that reign over his creation. That King
has sacrificed his own life in our place so that we could be free to enter
God's reign. Conversion, therefore, is submitting to this reign and allowing
Jesus to have his rightful place as King over one's life. And the unfinished
nature of the kingdom's arrival calls a person to seek the establishment of
more and more of this kingdom—in one's personal life and relationships,
in and through one's vocation, and in the world at large. It sets forth clearly
that following Jesus means signing on for an ongoing struggle to push
back the darkness and shine God's light in our world. The life of commitment, discipleship and mission flows much more clearly from understanding the gospel as that of the kingdom of God.

PART FIVE

THE COMMUNITY
OF THE KINGDOM

12

IT'S A COMMUNITY AFFAIR!

No one liked playing team sports with Jimmy. Whenever Jimmy joined a team, he'd whine about everything that didn't suit his particular tastes that day. "But I don't want to play third base—I want to be the pitcher!" "Why do I have to play with Sally? She's no good!" "I don't want to hit the volleyball that way—it hurts my hands!" "I want to be quarterback this time." "I'm tired. I don't want to play anymore." On and on it would go. And if Jimmy didn't get his way, he'd simply leave, which would leave us with uneven teams. It wasn't about "team" sports at all for Jimmy. For him, it was all about how *Jimmy* could have fun. All the rest of us were just extra pieces to be added or deleted or moved around to fit his desires.

Don't Christians sometimes sound the same way as they talk about churches? "I didn't like that church because the worship was too traditional for my taste." "The pastor's sermons just didn't do anything for me. They sort of left me flat." "I left that church because there was no one my age there. I just wasn't finding the fellowship that I need." "I'm thinking about switching churches because my church doesn't have air conditioning." "That church didn't fit me. I always left feeling bad about myself." "I'm not going to church these days. I couldn't find anything that fit me. So now I just read my Bible and pray on my own."

Too often, Christians approach their faith as an individualistic affair rather than a corporate one. And when they do consider the corporate side of faith, they judge it according to how it caters to their "needs": *How will this church help me get along as a Christian in this world? Will it give me the kind of teaching and fellowship that I need? Will it give me the kind of worship experience that will help me get closer to God?* The Christian life is viewed as a long race of *individuals* seeking to get to glory, and the church is a gas station where they fuel up—so if the gas station fails to provide the fuel, it only makes sense to find another one. Right?

Now, I am not saying that we don't need to evaluate churches by considering the pastor's sermons or the community life or the worship style. What is misguided, however, is the underlying assumption that church life is all about our individual relationship with God. We think that God sent Jesus so *each* of us could walk with God. We believe that God's plan is that people would *each* have a growing relationship with Jesus.

So the church is thought to exist in order to provide each of us the needed support and feeding so that we can keep growing in our relationship with God. After all, that's what's most important . . . at least that's what many Christians think. That's why people change churches. For them, once the church fails to live up to its purpose of providing the feeding and support needed to live out the Christian life, it's time to leave and find another one that will fulfill that purpose.

I believe that we need to rethink the nature and priority of the corporate body, the church. Throughout biblical history God has been gathering people together so that in them and through their life *together* he might work out his purposes for the world. It was never simply about God calling out an individual so that he or she might walk with God. No, when he called out individuals, it was so that each might play his or her part in the *people* of faith. We've gotten it backwards. We think that the church is there for us; in reality, we are there for the church.

Consider the corporate dimension of God's work through history. When God called Abram, he didn't do so just so that Abram would be blessed. No, God called Abram so that God might raise up through him a whole nation that would bless all the other nations of the world (Genesis 12:1-3).

Later, when God delivered Israel from slavery in Egypt, he gathered them together at Mt. Sinai in order to give them the law. He instructed them, through Moses, about what it meant to be his special people. The law was not a way for Israel to earn God's favor; rather, the law was meant to tell Israel how to live so that they would show the rest of the world what it meant to serve the living and true God. In his commentary on Exodus, Old Testament scholar John Durham writes that to be a holy nation meant to be "set apart, different than all other people by what they are and what they are becoming, a display people, a showcase to the world of how being in covenant relationship with Yahweh changes a people."[1]

So when God gave Israel laws about how to treat each other and how to treat the alien, the poor, the orphan and the widow, God did not mean to say, "OK, you do this; then you can get into heaven." Rather, he meant, "Do this to show the rest of the world what I am like and what I desire for humanity. Act in these ways so that the world knows that I desire loving relationships. Show them that I love the poor, the widow, the orphan and the alien." The law was meant to reveal the true and living God to the world *through his people.*

In the New Testament we find God continuing with his plan to gather a corporate people for himself. Consider Jesus' choice of *twelve* disciples. He did not choose ten, or eleven, or fifteen. No, he chose twelve. Do you remember another twelve from the Old Testament? Israel was founded on the twelve tribes of Israel descended from the twelve sons of Jacob, the patriarchs. Jesus regathered the twelve tribes of Israel, so to speak, when he called twelve disciples. Only now, under his reign, the reconstituted people of God would carry out God's purposes by the power of the Holy Spirit, freed from the power of sin and death. So God was continuing his purposes for Old Testament Israel but now through the church. That is probably why it was so important in Acts 1 for the early church to find a replacement for Judas Iscariot. They needed the disciples to number twelve.

Notice what Peter tells Christians in 1 Peter 2:9: "But you are a chosen race, a royal priesthood, a holy nation, God's own people, in order that you may proclaim the mighty acts of him who called you out of darkness into his marvelous light." Peter takes key images of Old Testament Israel—royal priesthood, holy nation, a people belonging to God—and uses them to refer to the New Testament church. What God was seeking to do in and through Israel is now continued in and through the church. So we, the church, are meant to be "set apart, different than all other people by what they are and what they are becoming, a display people, a showcase to the world of how being in covenant relationship with Yahweh changes a people."

For the church, as compared to Old Testament Israel, the fundamental reality that had changed was the kingdom of God. In Jesus, the kingdom of God had come, and the power of the Age to Come had been poured out in the Holy Spirit. It was not a community of God that had God's law to tell them how to live as God's special chosen people. Rather, it was a community of faith, of those who had God's Spirit indwelling them to teach and empower them to be God's special chosen people. No longer was it based on an ethnic community, the nation of Israel; now it was to spread and include all the nations of the earth.

So when we consider our involvement in the church, the local body of faith, we need to keep in mind a few things.

1. *The church, the corporate body of faith, is absolutely central to God's purposes.* It is not secondary to our individual relationships with Jesus. We dare not take a utilitarian approach to the community of faith, as if it exists only to feed and support us in our endeavor to grow in Christ. In fact, we live out the purposes to which we have been called in our salvation *only if* we live them out corporately with our brothers and sisters in the church. We cannot live out the Christian life the way God intended it if we live it out alone.

2. Part of what God is doing is revealing his love, justice and holiness through the church's life together. It is through the way we live together that the world can see and experience what it means to be connected to the living God. That's why conflict is often not enough reason to leave a church. It could be that it is through the hard work of reconciliation that God wants to reveal himself to you and to those around you. That's why it's not always appropriate to leave a church just because you don't "click" with the people there. Maybe there are ethnic, socioeconomic or age differences between you and most people in the church. God may want you to stay there and work through those differences with the people there. In the hard work of loving across those barriers, the transcendent, reconciling love of God can be seen by a watching world, and you benefit from experiencing the reconciling power of the Spirit binding you in love with your brothers and sisters in Christ.

3. God's purpose for the church is partly to model his values for the sake of a watching world. Too often I hear people complaining that their needs aren't being met in their church. I want to tell them that the community of faith is not meant to be simply a heavenly support group! No, the church is meant to be a community that witnesses to the truth and life of God. It's not just about our needs but about a whole world of people who need to see that God is alive and loves them. Through our individual lives and corporate life together, God is at work to show the world his love and power, his justice and truth. Often we become so self-absorbed with how the church is or is not meeting our needs that we forget that the church exists for the world. What I find is that as I turn my eyes to the needs of the world around me and seek to work with my church to reach out to the world, God meets me in my self-denial and sacrifice. My irritations and complaints about the church recede as I experience the heart of God reaching out to a lost world.

Let me quickly add that there *are* times when we are so deeply wounded and broken that it is nearly impossible to lift our eyes above the pain. It's not compassionate to simply tell a person to buck up and quit complaining. Sometimes life gets totally out of control—marriages falter, financial strains mount, depression deepens—and in times like these, when we are deeply burdened and overwhelmed, it is right to expect the church to be there for us. We need to let brothers and sisters into our need and let God meet us through them. And if the Christian body turns a blind eye to our pain, then maybe it is appropriate to find another Christian community that will provide the support that we desperately need.

What I am concerned about, however, is when Christians have these invisible checklists in their head of ways the church should meet their needs. And as they participate in the church week to week, they complain about those areas of need that their church isn't meeting. They slip into a mentality that the church is really about meeting one's needs rather than being a community who witnesses to the world about the transcendent love and power of Jesus Christ. It is in these situations that we need to refocus our vision to recognize that the church is, in part, a community that lives for those who are not yet in the community. It is not there just for us.

4. The power of the church is not in us but in the Spirit of God. The fundamental difference between Old Testament Israel and the New Testament church is that a new age has dawned, the age of the kingdom of God. And one defining mark of the new age of the kingdom is the Holy Spirit. The Holy Spirit is the power of the kingdom unleashed in our world. It is not as if the New Testament church just needs to do what Old Testament Israel failed to do. It's not as if Christians can just be more righteous in and of themselves. Of course not! Rather, we have been freed from the power of sin by the work of the cross and the life of the resurrection. As a result, the gift of the Holy Spirit has been given to us to empower us to be and do what God wants us to do as his special people.

In Romans, that is a key message of chapter 8:

> There is therefore now no condemnation for those who are in Christ
> Jesus. For the law of the Spirit of life in Christ Jesus has set you free from

the law of sin and of death. . . . For those who live according to the flesh set their minds on the things of the flesh, but those who live according to the Spirit set their minds on the things of the Spirit. To set the mind on the flesh is death, but to set the mind on the Spirit is life and peace. For this reason the mind that is set on the flesh is hostile to God; it does not submit to God's law—indeed it cannot, and those who are in the flesh cannot please God. But you are not in the flesh; you are in the Spirit, since the Spirit of God dwells in you. (vv. 1-2, 5-9)

So living out the kingdom witness as the community of faith demands that the church be animated not by its own power but by the power of the Holy Spirit. To do that, I believe, means that the church, both as individuals and as a corporate community, leans hard into the Spirit through spiritual disciplines like prayer, Scripture listening, and solitude. That's why they are called "spiritual" disciplines—they are disciplines that provide places and times for the Holy Spirit to work in us and equip us for kingdom service.

When we pray, we acknowledge our dependence on God as we lay our concerns in his lap and remove ourselves from the temptation to do it all in our own power. When we read the Scriptures, we listen to the Spirit's voice rather than trust in our own intuitions and ideas. When we pull out of the regular pace of life and retreat into periods of solitude, we quiet ourselves enough for the Spirit's whispering voice to cut through the mad rush of life and speak to us about what God wants us to do.

So as you think about living out the kingdom of God, remember that God's intent for the community of faith is to serve as *a Spirit-filled community before a watching world.* Living out the kingdom is not an individualistic endeavor. The kingdom is not primarily a confederation of people working out salvation on our own, and the corporate nature of the kingdom is not meant to support individuals as they live out their kingdom lives or to meet their needs. Nor is it a community of people seeking to live out the kingdom under their own power. Living out the kingdom demands that we all serve in a Spirit-filled community that is seeking to witness to the kingdom before a watching world.

What is your relationship with your local church or campus fellowship? Do you need to repent of an individualistic approach to the Christian life and the Christian community? Are you committed to living out the life of the kingdom in community the way God intends for you? Do you need to reconsider your attitude toward your Christian community? How can you help your Christian church or fellowship be a Spirit-filled community before a watching world?

13

THE KINGDOM
COMMUNITY

What does it mean for the community of faith to serve as a witness to its God in light of the kingdom of God?

As you remember, the good news of the kingdom of God is that the Age to Come has broken into history through the person and work of Jesus Christ. The blessings, power and justice of the future kingdom of God have reached back into the present and taken root in our world. History is moving toward the day when Jesus will return and establish God's kingdom in all of its fullness.

The church is the special community to which that age has come. We are the people who have been rescued from the dominion of darkness and brought into the kingdom of God. And we now experience the presence of God's kingdom by the power of the Holy Spirit who is at work among us. And we have the certain hope of the resurrection when, one day when Jesus returns, we will all be raised to new life, and all of creation will be freed from its bondage to death and decay.

The church, therefore, is to serve as a witness to that kingdom that is now-but-not-yet, that is present in part but still coming in full glory. In its corporate family life together, in the lives of its individual members and in what it does to reach out to an unbelieving world, the Christian community is supposed to reveal the present reality of the kingdom and point ahead to the certain hope of the future when the kingdom will come in all its fullness. Missiologist David Bosch writes that the church is "the sign of the dawning of the new age in the midst of the old, and as such the vanguard of God's new world. It is simultaneously acting as a pledge of the sure hope of the world's transformation at the time of God's final triumph and straining itself in all its activities to prepare the world for its coming destiny."[1] Another missiologist, Lesslie Newbigin, calls the church a "sign, instrument, and foretaste" of the kingdom.[2] Both Bosch and Newbigin understand the nature of the church as it stands in relation to the gospel of the kingdom.

SIGN OF THE KINGDOM

Bosch and Newbigin talk about the church as a sign of the kingdom's presence right in the midst of the Old Age of sin and death. As the world continues to run its course in its confusion and destruction, the church is supposed to be a beacon of light in the darkness. Bosch calls it the "vanguard of God's new world." The world is supposed to see in the church a glimpse of what God's reign is all about—its love and compassion, its justice and truth. As God does battle against Satan to reclaim his world, the church is a beachhead where God's power has taken hold. As men and women choose to follow Jesus and band together for the gospel, the forces of the Spirit come and plant the flag of God's reign as they push back the forces of sin and death.

As we have seen, this is not simply about individual Christians witnessing to God's kingdom but about the church's witness through its corporate life together. It is not simply a community of witnesses but a witnessing community.* As the church lives together by the

---

*InterVarsity Christian Fellowship's national purpose statement is built around a call to "establish and advance witnessing communities of students and faculty."

power of God's Spirit, our community life testifies to the rest of the world that God is really here among us establishing his reign of love and peace.

That's what happened at the birth of the church in Acts. The kingdom of God had come through Jesus, and the power of the kingdom was poured out on the church as the Spirit came to rest on God's people. Peter explained that the pouring out of the Spirit was a sign that the Age to Come had arrived. The Jesus who was crucified was revealed to be Lord and Messiah through his resurrection from the dead. Therefore, Peter appealed to the crowd to repent and believe in Jesus to receive the Holy Spirit and the forgiveness of sins. As a result, about three thousand were saved that day, and they joined together in community. Acts 2:42-47 describes that community:

> They devoted themselves to the apostles' teaching and fellowship, to the breaking of bread and the prayers. Awe came upon everyone, because many wonders and signs were being done by the apostles. All who believed were together and had all things in common; they would sell their possessions and goods and distribute the proceeds to all, as any had need. Day by day, as they spent much time together in the temple, they broke bread at home and ate their food with glad and generous hearts, praising God and having the goodwill of all the people. And day by day the Lord added to their number those who were being saved.

Christians often turn to this passage as a model of what Christian community is supposed to be. So they consider what activities and characteristics ought to mark a godly Christian community. That is all well and good, but what is often missing is an understanding of the kingdom dynamic at work. As people looked at this community, they saw a flesh and blood sign of the presence of the kingdom of God. God had poured out the Spirit of the kingdom on God's people in Acts 1; in Acts 2, by that Spirit God's reign was embodied by God's people before a watching world.

Alex had only bad experiences with Christians prior to coming to our campus group. All he saw was hypocrisy. Certain friends went to church and claimed to be Christians but lived as if God did not exist. In fact, some of these "Christians" were the most immoral of his friends. In our fellowship he met Becky, who reached out to Alex in friendship. As Alex got to know Becky, it became very clear to him that Becky's faith in Jesus was not just a Sunday event but something that pervaded her life. She naturally talked about her relationship with Jesus when talking to her friends. She was honest with Alex about what she believed. And she was very active in the campus fellowship. Soon Alex was going to a small group Bible discussion that Becky had started so that her non-Christian friends could come and honestly talk about spiritual things. Before long, Alex was coming regularly to our weekly meetings of worship and teaching and going to church each week with Becky. When I met Alex at an outreach one day, he told me, "Yeah, I really had a hard time with Christians who said one thing but didn't live up to what they said. But Becky and her friends, they just aren't like that. I've never seen such *nice* people! And there's just something about this group! It's as if *God* is here!" It was only a matter of time before Alex decided to follow Jesus.

When non-Christians get involved in a Spirit-filled community of faith, they start seeing and experiencing something that powerfully affects them. In my campus ministry, I can think of names like Nikki, Niven, Evan, Eileen, Chung Yu, Kevin, Sharon, and the list goes on. Many of them began by asking all of the hard questions that kept them from believing that Christianity could be true—for example, "How can there be only one way to God?" or "What about all the suffering and evil in the world?" After being involved in friendships and community life with us, many of them experienced something they had never experienced before: the kingdom of God. They saw God's love as Christians loved and sacrificed for each other. They sensed something transcendent as they watched Christians respond to God together in worship. This is the Christian community in action, serving as a sign of the presence of the kingdom.

As we lean hard on the Holy Spirit and his power, we can live out the life of the kingdom before a watching world. We, the church, are meant to be a sign of the present and coming kingdom of God.

FORETASTE OF THE KINGDOM

When I go home to visit my parents, my mom usually cooks me something good for dinner. I just love it when I can go to Mom and Dad's to eat sukiyaki or curry rice or some other Japanese dish. As dinnertime approaches, I begin to smell the sumptuous scents of Japanese food wafting from the kitchen. My mouth begins to water and my stomach begins to gurgle as I anticipate my mother's cooking. Dinnertime has not arrived yet. It is still on its way. But those smells . . . boy, I can't wait.

The Christian church is supposed to be a foretaste of that coming day when the kingdom will arrive in all of its fullness. Like those smells wafting over to me from my mom's kitchen, the church is supposed to be a foretaste of the incredible banquet of the kingdom of God. As the world sees and experiences the partial presence of the kingdom in and through the church, they get a foretaste of what it will be like when Jesus returns to restore all of creation.

As non-Christians experience the love of God in our campus fellowships, they get a taste of the incredible community life that awaits those who put their faith in Jesus and who will one day find a home in the kingdom of God. As they see the church stand for justice and compassion, they get a glimpse of where God is taking history, to a time when justice will reign and all people will be cared for. When the church binds up people's wounds and comforts the mourners, the world catches a glimpse of the time when God will wipe away every tear.

Rather than just another club on campus or another local gathering of people, the church is something special. We are God's chosen people in whom the Age to Come has taken root. As the Spirit enlivens our love and worship and empowers our truthtelling and actions, we give off the fragrance of the coming kingdom of God. We give people real tastes of the goodness, justice, power and mercy that will one day mark God's beneficent reign when Jesus returns and sets all things right.

INSTRUMENT OF THE KINGDOM

The corporate nature of the kingdom is vital in understanding our role as instruments of the kingdom. Not only must we seek to serve God's kingdom as individuals; as corporate bodies of faith, we also need to enact and sponsor activities that serve the kingdom of God.

One thing that attracted me to my church is how it continually seeks to balance a biblical faith with social involvement. While the pastoral staff and leadership seek to stay true to the Scriptures and call people to personal faith in Jesus, they also move the church to be active in the community for the sake of the poor and needy. The church regularly sponsors a soup kitchen on Saturdays; they have started a school for children of working parents from poorer families who need child-care; they have a church-and-society team that sponsors forums on issues like welfare and education; and they have intentionally developed sister church relationships with an African American church, an Arab Christian church in Palestine, a church in Haiti and an African church in Burkina Faso, in order that the congregation may stay in touch with issues of poverty and injustice as experienced by communities far different from most of the congregation's experiences.

A powerful statement is made when a church community as a corporate body acts in ways that advance the kingdom of God. It's not just that certain individuals from the church are doing kingdom-focused activities but that a whole church has put its institutional force toward seeking the kingdom of God. I believe this speaks loudly and distinctively in a way that the work of individuals does not.

I think of the Asian American fellowship of InterVarsity on my campus, Northwestern University. A number of the students went on a spring break urban project and worked alongside a ministry in a Hispanic neighborhood in Chicago called Grace and Peace. After their time there, some of the students challenged the whole fellowship to begin an ongoing relationship with Grace and Peace to serve its ministry. As a result, the students provided needed supplies for the ministry's children's programs; one student helped gather old computers and computer parts from the fellowship and then worked to refurbish them to give to Grace and Peace; and on particular Saturdays, they planned times for the fellowship to go there to lend manpower to Grace and Peace's building efforts. As I watched this unfold before me, I was deeply impressed by the statement being made. An Asian American fellowship crosses an ethnic barrier *as a corporate community.* Then they develop a kingdom agenda ministry program *as a corporate community.*

In the past, I have seen Christian students get excited about various opportunities for ministry. And what usually happens is that that one student ends up getting involved alone or gets a few friends to join in. While this does make a good witness to the kingdom of God, an entirely different sort of witness emerges when a whole community acts together as a witness to the kingdom. What the Asian American fellowship did spoke loudly and distinctly because it was done as a fellowship and not as a few individuals. My hope is that the Asian American fellowship will continue to develop programs *as a corporate community* that will speak loudly to a watching world about the King's agenda of peace and justice.

How is your church or fellowship doing as a sign, foretaste and instrument of the kingdom? What do you need to be praying for as you pray for your church? What role is God calling you to play to help your fellowship be a sign, foretaste and instrument of the kingdom?

Conclusion

When the gospel and the Christian life are about individuals, then the Christian community gets pushed aside as just another tool in the utility belt of faith. Rather than having vibrant communities of witness to testify to the presence and coming of the kingdom of God, we get individual believers who have lost their way and have gone off living a solitary

Christian life. If we do gather together in community, many of us stay only as long as our needs are met and our spiritual stomachs are fed. God wants to change the world through the church, but many believers look to the church as a means of fulfilling their own needs.

The gospel is about God's work to reclaim all of creation, and the Christian life is to be lived out in a Spirit-filled community before a watching world. Is it not time for us to wake up from our individualism and get on board with God's plan?

PART SIX

THE WAY
OF THE KINGDOM

14

THE WAY OF
THE CROSS

"Trust me, trust me." My friend-turned-navigator was telling me how to get to our destination, but I wasn't so sure about the directions. "Just turn left here and go straight. We'll hit a blacktop road in about a mile that will take us right where we want to go." *Left and straight here?!* I thought. My internal compass was crying out frantically in protest. I just knew that we were going in the wrong direction. But then again, my friend had come here before and claimed that he knew the way. This was my first time to have come this way.

Have you ever had to get to a destination via directions that took you through rarely traveled backwoods roads, in counterintuitive directions that made you feel as if you were going the wrong way? That's what the way of the kingdom is like, and that's why it's often hard to know which way to go as we walk the way of the kingdom. Many, I'm afraid, give up on the directions altogether and look for their own way.

When Jesus began his earthly ministry, many different voices claimed to know the way of the expected kingdom of God. They claimed that if you followed their way, you would eventually find the kingdom.

There were separatists, like the Essenes (many think the group that left us the Dead Sea Scrolls in Qumran was composed of Essenes). They pulled out of society in order to stay holy and wait for God to come crashing down on the world with fire and judgment. They thought that the world was so hopelessly lost, the religious and political power structures so corrupt, that reform was a lost cause. They pulled out of mainstream Jewish society into their own religious enclaves to wait for the kingdom. The rest of the world be damned. The way of the kingdom for these people was separation and waiting.

Then there were the zealots. With religious zeal, they passionately wanted the kingdom of God to come, so they sought to bring it through force and insurrection. One group became known for their assassinations by stabbing. Their name, the *Sicarii*, comes from a word that means "dagger." (I've even heard conjecture that Judas Iscariot came from this group, based on the similarity between *Iscariot* and *Sicarii*.) In the midst of a large crowd, the assassin would sneak up from behind and stab the target with a short dagger. Then he would stealthily sneak away before anyone would notice, and the victim would crumple to the ground. Periodically, other revolutionary groups would spring up with hopes of overthrowing the establishment in order to establish the kingdom. The time of history Jesus stepped into was volatile with revolutionary uprisings. The way of the kingdom for these people was revolution and insurrection.

Then there was Jesus.

Jesus came announcing that the kingdom of God was at hand, so all eyes were on him to see what he would do. Would he foment revolution? Would he pull people away into the desert? What would this Jesus do to bring the kingdom? Little did they realize just how wrong all their expectations were.

At first, the excitement must have been tremendous. Here was this man claiming to bring the kingdom, and everywhere he went people were healed, demons were cast out and forgiveness of sins was pronounced for the poor and outcast. And when he taught, his words were packed with power. The Scriptures tell us that the people were amazed at his teaching because he taught with such authority, unlike the scribes and Pharisees. There was something extraordinary about this man!

But soon, as his closest followers continued to walk the way after him, this Jesus started talking about suffering and death. He predicted that the chief priests and elders would arrest him, persecute him and put him to death—and oddly, he also predicted that he would rise from the dead. Now they knew that Jesus often spoke at a higher level than what they understood, so they wondered what he meant by "rising from the dead" (Mark 9:10). And they likely wondered how Jesus' words fit into their expectation that he was bringing the kingdom of God.

Jesus started telling them that to follow him meant to go after him into suffering and death. He said things like, "If any want to become my followers, let them deny themselves and take up their cross and follow me. For those who want to save their life will lose it, and those who lose their life for my sake, and for the sake of the gospel, will save it" (Mark 8:34-35). What does a cross have to do with the kingdom of God? After all, when people were nailed to a cross it meant that their attempts to fight for the kingdom had ended in failure. This was definitely *not* the way to the kingdom. How could it be?

It is easy for us to overlook the utter confusion and devastation of the cross when we stand on this side of Easter. But for Jesus' first followers, every ounce of hope and promise died with Jesus up on that cross. As far as they knew, it was the end of the story. All their dreams of the kingdom of God were gone. After all, who would have thought that the kingdom of God would come through *death* and through a *cross?* If anything, the kingdom should come *in spite* of the cross, not *through* the cross. This was definitely not the expected way into the glorious kingdom of God. That's why Paul writes that the message of Christ crucified was a stumbling block to Jews and foolishness to Gentiles (1 Corinthians 1:23).

Yet this *was* the way of the kingdom. This was the only way in which the kingdom of God would come. This was the way the true kingdom would come to reclaim a creation in bondage due to human sin. This was the only way that humanity's sin would be atoned for. Unbeknownst to all, this was God's plan to pay for the sin of humanity and to free creation for the Age to Come. This was the way of the kingdom.

When we talk about advancing the kingdom, the very word *kingdom* conjures up images of conquest and power. And as we think about how we establish God's kingdom, it would be easy for us to seek power as the way to do it. History shows us that the church has often strayed from the way of the cross and picked up the sword as the means to establish God's kingdom. The Crusades, the Inquisition, European colonialism—the church often forgot that the King of the kingdom came not to "take over" but to give his life away as a ransom for many. Even today, it is disconcerting to me when Christians wave their fists in the air against the world's ungodliness and talk about *forcing* the "pagans" to shape up. They seek societal and political power not to love and serve but to coerce the world to do what they think is right. If we are not careful, we will walk down the same road that the insurrectionists and zealots did during Jesus' day—seeking the kingdom through insurrection and power. All the while, the true King of the kingdom is walking down a different road, the road leading to a cross.

The other temptation we face is to retreat from the world out of fear of contamination. We pull back into our Christian huddles and hide from the sin and evil of the outside world. Seeking the kingdom of God in this context really has nothing to do with the rest of the world; it's all about us keeping ourselves in line. The rest of the world is going down the tubes anyway, so why bother changing it? Like the separatists, we set up our own mini-Christian society so as not to rub shoulders with the world. We see to our own education, we socialize only with one another, and we relate to those outside our communities only when necessary.

We forget that our King chose not to stay in the comfort and safety of his divine community, the Trinity, but to enter our world, become one of us, love us, live among us and go to the cross to die for us. The separatists were waiting for their king to bring the kingdom, yet when he came they didn't even know him. They, too, had walked down the wrong road. Their King was walking down the road of the cross while they were busy sticking to their road of separation and isolation.

For Jesus, the way of the kingdom was to give his life away. Out of love for his Father and for us, Jesus set his face for Jerusalem to suffer and die. It was not about forcing a lost world to believe or retreating from that world to stay pure. It was about love and sacrifice. It was about giving his life away so that others might truly live. This was the way of the kingdom for Jesus, and it is also the way for us. Now Jesus calls us to follow after him . . . on the way of the cross.

THE PATH MARKED OUT FOR US

As we seek to serve the advancing kingdom of God, there is a path marked out for us, a road that's already been trod. It is the way of the cross. It is following Jesus along the pathway of love, self-sacrifice and obedience to the Father.

Hebrews 12:1-2 talks about the race of faith:

> Let us also lay aside every weight and the sin that clings so closely, and let us run with perseverance the race that is set before us, looking to Jesus the pioneer and perfecter of our faith, who for the sake of the joy that was set before him endured the cross, disregarding its shame, and has taken his seat at the right hand of the throne of God.

Jesus is the "pioneer" of our faith, the trailblazer, marking out the pathway of faith for the rest of us to follow. Where there was no pathway to God open to us due to our sin, Jesus blazed a trail by providing the perfect sacrifice for our sin and conquering death at the cross and resurrection. So Jesus turns to us and says, "If any want to become my followers, let them deny themselves and take up their cross daily and follow me. For those who want to save their life will lose it, and those who lose their life for my sake will save it" (Luke 9:23-24). It's not that he calls us to die for the world's sins—only Jesus could and did do that. Rather, the pathway is one of trust, obedience, renunciation and sacrifice. It's a pathway of giving up life, trusting that in the end God will give true life. It's about loving others enough to sacrifice self and put your life into God's hands.

Paul knew this path. That's why his letters show that the way of the cross was woven into the very fabric of his thinking. In writing to the Corinthians, for example, he said, "For I decided to know nothing among you except Jesus Christ, and him crucified" (1 Corinthians 2:2). Michael Gorman explains that "'to know' means something like 'to experience and to announce in word and deed.'"[1] Paul repeatedly alludes to the shape of the cross in his life (emphasis mine in all quotes):

> For while we live, we are always being *given up to death* for Jesus' sake, so that the life of Jesus may be made visible in our mortal flesh. So death is at work in us, but life in you. (2 Corinthians 4:11-12)

> May I never boast of anything except *the cross of our Lord Jesus Christ*, by which the world has been crucified to me, and I to the world. (Galatians 6:14)

> I carry *the marks of Jesus* branded on my body. (Galatians 6:17)

> I want to know Christ and the power of his resurrection and the *sharing of his sufferings* by becoming like him in his death. (Philippians 3:10)

Michael Gorman's book *Cruciformity: Paul's Narrative Spirituality of the Cross* looks through Paul's letters and finds the shape of the cross in all aspects of Paul's life, even when the cross is not explicitly mentioned. In his concluding remarks Gorman writes,

> Paul wanted his life and ministry to tell a story, a story that corresponded to the master story of Christ's self-emptying, self-giving faith, love, power, and hope. That master story provided patterns for life that created constant occasions for a wide variety of analogous acts of faith, love, power,

and hope. The apostle's mission was to approximate a faithful retelling, in his life, of that story, and to create a series of communities that, together and individually, would be a living exegesis of the same story. Paul's cruciform mission continues today.[2]

This cruciform life of Paul's was not just for Paul. As Gorman states, Paul's ministry was about creating churches that lived out the cruciform life corporately and individually. In the same way that Jesus calls us to pick up our crosses, Paul calls us to live out the cross as well.

Notice, for example, what Paul says in Philippians 2:3-4:

> Do nothing from selfish ambition or conceit, but in humility regard others as better than yourselves. Let each of you look not to your own interests, but to the interests of others.

And notice how, immediately following these words, Jesus and his cross become the example:

> Let the same mind be in you that was in Christ Jesus,
>   who, though he was in the form of God,
>   did not regard equality with God
>   as something to be exploited,
>   but emptied himself,
>   taking the form of a slave,
>   being born in human likeness.
>   And being found in human form,
>   he humbled himself
>   and became obedient to the point of death—
>   even death on a cross. (vv. 5-8)

The model of Jesus and his cross was not just something that marked Paul's life; it was something Paul thought ought to mark the lives of people who follow Jesus.

LIVES OF CRUCIFORMITY

What does it really mean for us to follow in the way of the cross as we seek to advance God's kingdom? Gorman, after thorough analysis of Paul's letters, lays out some guidelines that help us understand more clearly what the way of the cross, or what he calls *cruciformity,* means. I've selected parts from the book that I think will be helpful for us as we consider the meaning of the way of the cross.

Trust and self-sacrifice.

> Cruciform faith refers to a dynamic of initial and ongoing narrative posture before God. . . . It is a "posture," for lack of a better word, in which the believer abandons all ultimate commitments save one, thus putting his or her complete trust in the God revealed in Christ's cross and giving him- or herself completely to the plan and mission of that same God.[3]

For Jesus, the cross was the supreme event whereby he gave himself completely to the plan and mission of the Father. He "became obedient to the point of death—even death on a cross" (Philippians 2:8). We will continually be faced with decisions where we have to choose whether we will trust God or not. And they will often be costly.

Deborah came to Northwestern University from a middle-class upbringing in the South. Even though she has lived in Chicago for several years, every once in a while her Mississippi "y'all" still slips out. During her time at Northwestern, God began to open her eyes to the needs of the poor and to the systemic injustices that help keep people poor. She read books about race, poverty and injustice; she participated in an InterVarsity urban project in Chicago; and she volunteered at a local tutoring facility for inner-city kids. By the time she graduated, she felt God's call to serve the poor in the city and found a job helping to serve underprivileged single mothers.*

After a few years of renting an apartment, she and her husband, Emmett, considered whether they should buy a home in a poorer neighbor-

---

*Her organization is called New Moms.

hood in Chicago. This would put Deborah right in the neighborhood of the families she was serving. The decision had costly implications. Because they wanted to eventually have children, issues like education, health care and safety were major areas of concern. They looked at the homes of some of their peers living out in the suburbs and imagined what it would look like if their kids grew up there. Yet they knew that God was calling Deborah to the city. And they knew, too, that if they postponed the decision until after they had children or after they lived in suburbia for a while, it would be even harder to move into the city. So they set their faces toward the city and looked for a home in Humboldt Park, a largely Hispanic neighborhood. Deborah shared with me how she invited a friend from the Humboldt Park community to drive around with her to help her choose a home to put a bid on. Her friend would give the inside scoop on some of the homes as they drove around: "Nope, not that one. Way too much gang activity down this block." "Lots of drug activity around the corner; I wouldn't choose that one." Deborah and Emmett eventually bought a home that fit their price range, and they now live in Humboldt Park.

As we hear God's call on our life and understand his kingdom purposes, will we trust God with our life and take steps of obedience? Will we trust that God loves us and will take care of us as we follow his purposes? Will we trust God with our career choices even at the cost of apparent financial security? Will we trust God in terms of a spouse even if it means remaining single? When faced with choices of integrity at work, will we trust God even if that means risking possible promotion or economic advantage?

As you consider your life today, what does it look like for you to put your complete trust in God and give yourself completely to his plan and mission? What is the Spirit of God highlighting for you right now?

The way of the cross is about *trust* and *self-sacrifice*. With our eyes looking up to the Father, the way of the kingdom is to say Jesus' prayer, "Not my will but yours, Father."

Love and service.

> Cruciform love is others-centered and community driven. . . . Cruciform
> love resists the temptation to make myself the focus of everything, even
> of my spirituality. Cruciform love refuses to exercise rights, powers, priv-
> ileges, spiritual gifts, and so forth, if their use will do me good but some-
> one else, or a community of which I am a part of, harm. It liberates me
> from myself and for the other.[4]

Jesus was God incarnate, yet he "did not regard equality with God as
something to be exploited" (Philippians 2:6). For our sake, Jesus voluntarily chose to give up what he deserved. Cruciform love is not to view
ourselves as lowly worms who deserve to be taken advantage of. It's not
to let go of rights, privileges and power for the sake of others because
in Christ we are nothing. No, Jesus knew who he was. He knew that he
was God's Son, but out of love and obedience he *voluntarily* let go of the
rights, privileges and power that he deserved so that we might live. As
2 Corinthians 8:9 says, "For your sake he became poor." In the same
manner, the way of the cross demands that we, out of love, follow Jesus'
pattern and voluntarily give up what we deserve so that others may live
and benefit.

As a staff worker with InterVarsity, I am awestruck by some of our do-
nors. I know of so many people who intentionally live with less so that
they might give to our campus ministry. They do this because they want
students to meet Jesus and be raised up as spiritual influencers for the
kingdom of God.

As I encounter people, whether in groups or individually, it is quite
easy for me to consider, *How can I position myself in this encounter in order
to avoid getting uncomfortable or to accomplish my agenda or to gain the respect of others?* Granted, I would never say that out loud—but if I am not
careful, my mind races toward those questions. Cruciform love demands
that I put a stop to such internal maneuvering and instead ask how I can
position myself in order to serve the needs of others and the community.

As you look around at your relationships and your church or fellowship community, where are you tempted to make yourself the focus rather than the needs of others? How can you retrain your mind to think about serving others rather than seeking your own welfare and prestige? In which situations and relationships do you need to invite God's help so that you live out a cruciform love?

The way of the cross is *love* and *service*. With our eyes looking outward at the people around us, the way of the kingdom is to serve others rather than ourselves.

Downward mobility.

> Cruciform love motivates people with status, privilege, power, and/or money to be downwardly mobile. . . . Cruciform love does not motivate people to make decisions or take action based on how the decision or action will impress those of like or higher socioeconomic status. Rather, it motivates people to decide and to act on the basis of the needs of others with less socioeconomic status.[5]

Jesus, being God, rather than exploiting his position as God's Son, "emptied himself, taking the form of a slave, being born in human likeness. And being found in human form, he humbled himself and became obedient to the point of death—even death on a cross" (Philippians 2:7-8). It's interesting to note that, according to this passage, Jesus took several "steps" down in order to deal with our need for salvation. As God's Son he became human—one step down. He did not just become human but took the form of a slave—two steps down. He humbled himself to the point of giving his life up—three steps down. He didn't just die, but he willingly died on the cross as a treasonous criminal—four steps down. Jesus was clearly "downwardly mobile." The way of the cross is about following the pattern of Jesus in his downward mobility.

Lewis Hsu works for Grady Memorial Hospital in Atlanta, Georgia. He explains how he views his role as a physician:

[I see myself as] an advocate for care of the indigent, care of the poor, in the urban type of place. . . . Many people have said the culture of Atlanta is business, and that's what everybody here is all about. And for medicine particularly these days, it's more of a corporate type of culture where we are not so much in a department, we're in a service line, and we are line workers, and we're very heavily oriented in medicine toward what is the profitability and things like that, even if we're in a nonprofit-type institution. So doing something which is for those who can't pay, who have no means ever to really recoup the payment, kind of goes against all that. And trying to influence medicine to still remember to take care of these who are not particularly desirable in a profit-making hospital or even a hospital that's trying to break even, is part of what I'm trying to do.[6]

In the broader society, the way of the kingdom asks us to consider those who have less privilege and economic status. I have to admit, there are times that it's easy to be Asian American. When I go into stores I am never followed because of suspicion that I'll rob the place. When I drive down the highway, I am never pulled over by the police without a clear reason. If I were to move into many white suburban neighborhoods, my neighbors would not likely be afraid of me or resent my presence there. Yet many of my African American and Latino brothers and sisters have to deal with such unfortunate realities all of the time.

It is much easier for me to stay quiet, avoid conflict and enjoy the privileges. Yet following Jesus and his cross demands that I become an advocate for those with less socioeconomic status or those who are treated unfairly. Following Jesus requires that I be concerned about issues that affect African Americans and Latinos, not just those that affect Asian Americans. The way of the kingdom calls me to love the poor and needy and work to empower them for social advancement.

As you look at your own status, whether at work, in church or in social circles, how can you live out cruciform love that is downwardly mobile? Where are you tempted to impress those higher on the scale than you (socially, economically and hierarchically) rather than to serve and empower those below you? What opportunities do you have to advocate for those less fortunate than you?

The way of the cross is about *downward mobility*. With our eyes looking out at those less fortunate, the way of the kingdom is to let go of rights and privileges in order to lift up those in need.

Inclusion and forgiveness.

> Cruciform love is inclusive. Cruciform love, continuing the story of God's love in Christ for all the world, includes all: believer and nonbeliever, Gentile and Jew, woman and man, friend and enemy. It is a love characterized not by "exclusion" but by "embrace."[7]

Jesus' love extended to the outcast, the sinner, the poor and oppressed. And at the cross the inclusiveness of that love extended to all humanity. As Paul wrote, "while we still were sinners Christ died for us. . . . While we were enemies, we were reconciled to God" (Romans 5:8, 10). As you look around at the people you relate to and your relationships, do you have a tendency to exclude? Are all of your friendships with people of the same ethnicity or socioeconomic status? Invite the Lord to help you take steps to live out the inclusive love of the cross toward people it is hard for you to love or relate to:

> More to the point, are there *enemies* in your life that need to be reconciled with?
>
> The story of the cross that we receive from Paul is first of all a story of how God treats enemies. Those who have come to know the love of God in Christ have experienced the love of One who has responded to enemies, not with vengeance or violence, but with unmerited love. To have faith in this God is thus to be embraced by such love; *to pass such love on to others is the only proof of having received it.*[8]

The way of the kingdom is about *inclusion* and *forgiveness*. With our eyes fixed on our enemies, the way of the kingdom is to say Jesus' prayer, "Father, forgive them, for they know not what they do" (see Luke 23:34).

CONCLUSION

We have been called to serve the advancing kingdom of God and embody it in our life both individually and corporately. Yet in our desire to serve and embody this kingdom, we are often tempted to bypass the way of our King and opt for other roads that are marked by coercion, self-promotion and self-protection. Yet the pathway has already been marked out for us. It is the way of the cross. It is the way of cruciformity. It is following the road Jesus walked as he obeyed his Father, loved the world and died for all humanity. Will you walk the way of the kingdom, the way of the cross?

15

HOPE

Imagine the scene: they had pinned all their hopes on him. Some had left their jobs (some *lucrative* jobs) in order to join in this man's venture. Others had left family and friends. Two of them had literally left their dad standing on the dock as they left their family fishing business to go after this man. All because they thought that this man could change the world. He seemed like he was someone trustworthy. He cared deeply for each of them. He took time to know them each by name. They had never experienced such deep love and care in their lives. He said some wonderful things and talked about how he had come to make the world brand new. What's more, he did some incredible things that backed up his talk. He healed sick people, cast out demons and even raised some dead people back to life!

But now all their hopes had been dashed. This man they trusted so much had been accused of being a terrorist. He had been tried and convicted in the courts and sentenced to death. And on this day he had been executed. All their hopes and dreams had been destroyed right before their eyes. They had left everything for him; now they had nothing left but broken dreams and fear for their lives. This man they trusted had been executed as a terrorist. How long would it take for the authorities to come after them?

So there they sat, huddled together in a secret room, one of them standing guard at the window.

This was what it must have been like for the eleven remaining disciples on the day that Jesus died. Jesus talked about the dawning of the kingdom of God. I'm sure they were all eagerly awaiting the fulfillment of Old Testament promises that God would decisively come to restore Israel and all of creation. But rather than victory, they faced total defeat as the corpse of their Messiah was laid to rest in a tomb. Jesus was dead.

Today as we follow the way of the cross, it can often get confusing and dark. For some, the pursuit of the kingdom leads them into times when it looks impossible. Tragedies hit, crises mount or life just does not work out as planned. Whatever the case, as some try to seek the kingdom they experience periods when it seems that all hope is lost, all the sacrifice was in vain—and they wonder whether all of this Jesus stuff was ever true to begin with. The temptation is to get disillusioned and just give up.

Yet the way of the cross is about resurrection, about hope even when all hope seems lost. As Jesus' disciples followed him to Jerusalem, they hit Good Friday, but Easter morning came. Not only was death overcome, but the cross, the very place of pain and agony, was the vehicle by which God's victory was won. Easter shows us that the way of the cross is about unexpected hope, about hope *after* death, about hope even when all hope seems gone.

The way of the cross sometimes leads us into those places where all we can do is hold on. We can't see our way forward, we are confused that God isn't doing what we expect, and we can't see any meaning for all the pain and frustration.

We were so sure that God was leading us. My wife had gained affirmation and recognition as a gifted teacher when she served on staff with me for InterVarsity. We decided that she should go to graduate school in biblical studies in order to be better equipped in her teaching. While in graduate school she excelled and won awards in her study of the Old Testament. Professors encouraged her toward doctoral work. She got into a prestigious doctoral program in ancient Near Eastern studies and then received full funding. She dreamed of teaching the Old Testament. She continued to excel in her doctoral studies despite the intense rigors of the program.

Now, however, this has all changed. At one point, the internal lid that covered the pain from the sexual abuse she experienced during childhood came off and the floodgates opened. The pain and agony of the healing process continues to be so intense that it is impossible for her to continue in her studies. She has had to drop out of the program altogether with no assurance that she can return. I see her immense library and wonder whether she'll ever go back to it.

This has sent my spiritual world into disarray. What is God doing? Or more pointedly, why isn't he doing anything? Where is he? Yet I am amazed at what is happening in my life. After three years, the situation for my wife is far from resolved. It continues to be a painful journey day after day. However, through it all I am being led into a deeper relationship with God that is hard to describe. I've realized that I cannot hold God in a box as if he must act the way I expect him to act.

I'm sure the disciples could not fathom that God would let his Son, the Messiah, be crucified. Surely God would prevent such a horrible end. When faced with a cross, my expectation, too, was that God would save me from it. Yet God has shown me that when I must face my cross, he will not always save me from it. *But* he is still good, and he will yet bring good from the very cross that I face. The cross of Jesus shows me this. A good and gracious God stood back while the world crucified his only Son, and Jesus' followers could not fathom how any of this was good. But now we know that our very salvation was won at that cross. Who would have guessed that this would happen?

As I face my own ordeal of walking with my wife through this pain, I've heard God continually challenge me to believe that he is good and that he loves me and my wife. And the resurrection of Jesus looms in my horizon as a beacon of hope assuring me that God will bring good from this. I know not at all how it will look, but he is good and is at work to work out his purposes in my life. In the same way that the resurrection was completely and utterly unforeseen, I know that I cannot predict what the future will look like. But he assures me that the future is good.

Following Jesus might take us into dark, lonely places where we can't see any light at the end of the tunnel. Yet, scary as it may be, resurrection is not about God coming in the nick of time to save the day but about God coming after the corpse is dead and buried. Sometimes God reaches in only when the darkness has gotten pitch black and *then* shows his resurrection power to bring good in the midst of evil and pain. The challenge is to keep holding on, believing in Jesus and his kingdom, and trusting that he will accomplish his purposes even if we can't see how. We must always do what we know is right and true before God even if it doesn't seem as if it produces results. It's about taking one more step forward even if it seems pointless. If you are in one of those places, please look at the cross and grab hold of the resurrection hope that is found in the Savior who went there.

We believe in a God who created a universe out of nothing, who brought life *after* death, who makes sinners into saints, who raised his Son, Jesus, after Jesus had been dead and buried. In the present, the future is not known. We might think we know what the future will bring, or we might think we know what cannot happen, but face it: we don't know. And in that sliver of not knowing is a whole realm of kingdom possibilities that only God knows. And it is through that sliver of possibilities that God does what no one would ever have imagined. We serve the God of resurrection.

CONCLUSION

The way of the cross is not an easy road. In fact, times will come when we can't figure it out anymore. We're seeking God, serving his purposes, and we wind up in situations that look impossible. God seems absent; we can't see how he can make things work out right. Yet this is the way of the cross . . . and resurrection. We must never forget that the path of the cross leads to and through the darkness of death, not around it. Yet the God that we follow is the God of resurrection. We must hang on and stay faithful for as long as it takes. For too many, the cross is just the symbol of our salvation and not the pathway of life. But for all who follow Jesus, he calls us to walk the way of the cross and experience the power and joy of the resurrection: "Indeed, we felt that we had received the sentence of death so that we would rely not on ourselves but on God who raises the dead. He who rescued us from so deadly a peril will continue to rescue us; on him we have set our hope that he will rescue us again" (2 Corinthians 1:9-10). Don't give up. Keep serving the King. Keep trusting that his kingdom is here in part and on its way. As Tony Campolo often says, "It's Friday, but Sunday's coming!"

CONCLUSION

I remember when I was a student in InterVarsity at Millikin University so many years ago. Jesus had caught hold of me; he filled me with a deep sense of his presence and broke my heart for a lost world. As a result, I was filled with an idealistic passion to go out and change the world.

Now, over a decade later, I look at my life and see quite a few changes. Now there are weighty responsibilities for family and finances; I've been through several painful ministry battles and accumulated scars in the process; I've watched marriages disintegrate; I've seen far too many people get disillusioned with God and walk away; physically, I watch as more and more of me gathers and bulges around my midsection. I don't have the energy I used to, so I marvel at college students who do all-nighters and think, *Did I really stay up all night like that?* This is not to say that I'm overweight and depressed—no, I've just grown up a bit, and I hope I'm a bit wiser. I've gained good experience, and I can see things a bit more clearly. But you know what?

I *still* want to change the world!

I am convinced that Jesus is the hope of the world and the lover of humanity. I am convinced that Jesus came to call us back home and that one day he will come to make all things new. I am convinced that even now Jesus is at work, through the Holy Spirit, changing the world and letting people in on the wonderful reality of the kingdom of God.

The kingdom of God. Understanding it has made all the difference in the world for me. It is my prayer that as you understand and seek the kingdom of God, you, too, will catch a renewed vision for what you can do to be a part of God's kingdom plan.

NOTES

Chapter 3: The Message of the Kingdom

[1]George Eldon Ladd, *The Gospel of the Kingdom* (Grand Rapids: Eerdmans, 1994), p. 19.

[2]Ibid., p. 22.

[3]C. S. Lewis, *The Lion, the Witch and the Wardrobe* (New York: Collier, 1950), pp. 95-118.

[4]N. T. Wright, *The Challenge of Jesus* (Downers Grove, Ill.: InterVarsity Press, 2001), p. 37.

[5]N. T. Wright discusses the diversity of beliefs in Judaism about the coming kingdom in *The New Testament and the People of God* (Minneapolis: Fortress, 1992), pp. 280-338.

Chapter 4: The Gospel of the Kingdom in Our Lives

[1]N. T. Wright, *The Challenge of Jesus* (Downers Grove, Ill.: InterVarsity Press, 2001), pp. 36-37.

[2]Mark Noll, *The Scandal of the Evangelical Mind* (Grand Rapids: Eerdmans, 1994), p. 51.

[3]James Sire, *Discipleship of the Mind* (Downers Grove, Ill.: InterVarsity Press, 1990), p. 94.

[4]Jennifer Su, "Sowing the Seed of Christianity," *Northwestern Magazine*, Summer 2002, <www.northwestern.edu/magazine/northwestern/summer2002/features/coverstory/sidebar4.htm>.

[5]Interview with Joel Gross, "Following Christ: IVCF Graduate & Faculty Ministries Conference, 2002" (Madison, Wis.: 2100 Productions), videorecording.

[6]Interview with Neil Shorthouse, "Following Christ: IVCF Graduate & Faculty Ministries Conference, 2002" (Madison, Wis.: 2100 Productions), videorecording.

Chapter 5: Where's the Kingdom?

[1]George Eldon Ladd, *The Gospel of the Kingdom* (Grand Rapids: Eerdmans, 1994), p. 55.

[2]For more information, see N. T. Wright, *The New Testament and the People of God* (Minneapolis: Fortress, 1992), pp. 170-81.

Chapter 6: The Tension

[1]The D-Day imagery comes from Oscar Cullmann, *Christ and Time* (Philadelphia: Westminster Press, 1964), p. 87.

[2]N. T. Wright, *The Challenge of Jesus* (Downers Grove, Ill.: InterVarsity Press, 2001), p. 143.

[3]George Eldon Ladd, *The Gospel of the Kingdom* (Grand Rapids: Eerdmans, 1994), p. 44.

[4]Gordon Fee, *God's Empowering Presence* (Peabody, Mass.: Hendrickson, 1994), p. 806.

[5]Michael Gorman, *Cruciformity* (Grand Rapids: Eerdmans, 2001), p. 320.

[6]Richard Hays, *The Moral Vision of the New Testament* (New York: HarperCollins, 1996), pp. 402-3.

Chapter 7: Living with the Tension

[1]Stanley Grenz, *Prayer: The Cry for the Kingdom* (Peabody, Mass.: Hendrickson, 1988), p. 41

Chapter 8: Seeing Stars
[1]Interview with Joel Gross, "Following Christ: IVCF Graduate & Faculty Ministries Conference, 2002" (Madison, Wis.: 2100 Productions), videorecording. This quote was edited out of the final product.

[2]Vinay Samuel and Chris Sugden, eds., *Mission as Transformation* (Oxford: Regnum, 1999), p. 40, emphasis added.

[3]"Wizard of Odds: Interview with Bishop Vaughn McLaughlin," *Leadership Journal* 24 (Spring 2003): 26.

Chapter 9: Rethinking the Mission
[1]Michael Emerson and Christian Smith, *Divided by Faith: Evangelical Religion and the Problem of Race in America* (New York: Oxford, 2000), p. 132.

[2]Interview with Seymour Williams, "Following Christ: IVCF Graduate & Faculty Ministries Conference, 2002" (Madison, Wis.: 2100 Productions), videorecording.

[3]Charles Malik, *A Christian Critique of the University* (Downers Grove, Ill.: InterVarsity Press, 1982), p. 100.

[4]Mark Noll, *The Scandal of the Evangelical Mind* (Grand Rapids: Eerdmans, 1994), p. 51.

[5]Ibid., pp. 235-36.

[6]Malik, *Christian Critique of the University*, p. 100.

[7]Peter Kreeft, *How to Win the Culture War* (Downers Grove, Ill.: InterVarsity Press, 2002), p. 54.

Chapter 10: Living in the Matrix
[1]John F. Alexander, *The Secular Squeeze: Reclaiming Christian Depth in a Shallow World* (Downers Grove, Ill.: InterVarsity Press, 1993), pp. 15, 16.

Chapter 12: It's a Community Affair!
[1]John Durham, *Exodus*, Word Biblical Commentary (Nashville: Thomas Nelson, 1987), 3:263.

Chapter 13: The Kingdom Community
[1]David Bosch, *Transforming Mission: Paradigm Shifts in Mission* (New York: Orbis, 1996), p. 169.

[2]Lesslie Newbigin, *Foolishness to the Greeks* (Grand Rapids: Eerdmans, 1986), p. 124.

Chapter 14: The Way of the Cross
[1]Michael Gorman, *Cruciformity: Paul's Narrative Spirituality of the Cross* (Grand Rapids: Eerdmans, 2001), p. 1.

[2]Ibid., p. 400.

[3]Ibid., p. 387.

[4]Ibid., p. 389.

[5]Ibid., p. 390.

[6]Interview with Lewis Hsu, "Following Christ: IVCF Graduate & Faculty Ministries Conference, 2002" (Madison, Wis.: 2100 Productions), videorecording.

[7]Gorman, *Cruciformity*, p. 391.

[8]Ibid., p. 392, emphasis added.

BIBLIOGRAPHY

Abraham, William. *The Logic of Evangelism*. Grand Rapids: Eerdmans, 1989.

Alexander, John F. *The Secular Squeeze: Reclaiming Christian Depth in a Shallow World*. Downers Grove, Ill.: InterVarsity Press, 1993.

Bosch, David. *Transforming Mission: Paradigm Shifts in Mission*. New York: Orbis, 1996.

Cullmann, Oscar. *Christ and Time*. Philadelphia: Westminster Press, 1964.

Durham, John. *Exodus*. Word Biblical Commentary 3. Nashville: Thomas Nelson, 1987.

Emerson, Michael, and Christian Smith. *Divided by Faith: Evangelical Religion and the Problem of Race in America*. New York: Oxford University Press, 2000.

Fee, Gordon. *God's Empowering Presence*. Peabody, Mass.: Hendrickson, 1994.

Gorman, Michael. *Cruciformity: Paul's Narrative Spirituality of the Cross*. Grand Rapids: Eerdmans, 2001.

Grenz, Stanley. *Prayer: The Cry for the Kingdom*. Peabody, Mass.: Hendrickson, 1988.

Hays, Richard. *The Moral Vision of the New Testament*. New York: HarperCollins, 1996.

Ladd, George Eldon. *The Gospel of the Kingdom: Scripture Studies in the Kingdom of God*. 1959. Reprint, Grand Rapids: Eerdmans, 1994.

Ladd, George Eldon. *A Theology of the New Testament*. 1974. Reprint, Grand Rapids: Eerdmans, 1987. Revised and updated by Donald Hagner in 1993.

Lewis, C. S. *The Lion, the Witch and the Wardrobe*. New York: Collier, 1950.

Malik, Charles. *A Christian Critique of the University*. Downers Grove, Ill.: InterVarsity Press, 1982.

Newbigin, Lesslie. *Foolishness to the Greeks*. Grand Rapids: Eerdmans, 1986.

Noll, Mark. *The Scandal of the Evangelical Mind*. Grand Rapids: Eerdmans, 1994

Samuel, Vinay, and Chris Sugden, ed *Mission as Transformation*. Oxford: Regnum, 1999.

Sire, James. *Discipleship of the Mind.* Downers Grove, Ill.: InterVarsity Press, 1990.

Wenham, David. *The Parables of Jesus.* Downers Grove, Ill.: InterVarsity Press, 1989.

Wright, N. T. *The Challenge of Jesus.* Downers Grove, Ill.: InterVarsity Press, 2001.

Wright, N. T. *The New Testament and the People of God.* Minneapolis: Fortress, 1992.

ADDITIONAL RESOURCES

Beale, G. K. "The New Testament and New Creation." In *Biblical Theology: Retrospect and Prospect.* Edited by Scott J. Hafemann. Downers Grove, Ill.: InterVarsity Press, 2002.

Bright, John. *The Kingdom of God.* Nashville: Abingdon, 1989.

France, R. T. *Jesus the Radical.* Leicester, England: Inter-Varsity Press, 1989.

Goldsworthy, Graeme. *According to Plan: The Unfolding Revelation of God in the Bible.* Downers Grove, Ill.: InterVarsity Press, 2002.

Malik, Charles. *The Two Tasks.* Westchester, Ill.: Cornerstone, 1980.

Newbigin, Lesslie. *Sign of the Kingdom.* Grand Rapids: Eerdmans, 1980.

Wright, N. T. *Jesus and the Victory of God.* Minneapolis: Fortress, 1996.

ABOUT THE AUTHOR

Allen Wakabayashi has an M.A. from Wheaton College Graduate School in Missions/Intercultural Studies, has studied at Trinity Evangelical Divinity School and is currently pursuing graduate studies in theology at Loyola University in Chicago. He has served on various campuses with InterVarsity Christian Fellowship since 1989. Currently he oversees the undergraduate ministries of InterVarsity at Northwestern University in Evanston, Illinois, where they have three growing groups—multiethnic InterVarsity, Greek InterVarsity and Asian American Christian ministry. He has been married to his wife, Diane, since 1992. And they enjoy their dogs—Abby, Sheba, Tiberius and Josephus.